Deep Water

Development and Change in Pacific Village Fisheries

Development, Conflict, and Social Change

Scott Whiteford and William Derman
Michigan State University
Series Editors

Deep Water

Development and Change in Pacific Village Fisheries

Margaret Critchlow Rodman

Westview Press
BOULDER & LONDON

Development, Conflict, and Social Change

All photographs in this text are courtesy of the author.

The cover illustration features Vanuatu fish traps.

This Westview softcover edition is printed on acid-free paper and bound in softcovers that carry the highest rating of the National Association of State Textbook Administrators, in consultation with the Association of American Publishers and the Book Manufacturers' Institute.

Published in 1989 in the United States of America by Westview Press, Inc., 5500 Central Avenue, Boulder, Colorado 80301, and in the United Kingdom by Westview Press, Inc., 13 Brunswick Centre, London WC1N 1AF, England

Library of Congress Cataloging-in-Publication Data
Rodman, Margaret.
  Deep water : development and change in Pacific village fisheries/
Margaret Critchlow Rodman.
    p. cm.—(Development, conflict, and social change series)
  Bibliography: p.
  Includes index.
  ISBN 0-8133-7540-1
  1. Rural development—Vanuatu—Case studies. 2. Fisheries—
Vanuatu—Case studies. 3. Economic development projects—Vanuatu—
Case studies. I. Title. II. Series.
HN935.Z9C67 1989
307.7'2'09934—dc19   88-27900
                                                                             CIP

Printed and bound in the United States of America

The paper used in this publication meets the requirements of the American National Standard for Permanence of Paper for Printed Library Materials Z39.48-1984.

10   9   8   7   6   5   4   3   2

For Bill,
my anchor to windward

CONTENTS

ILLUSTRATIONS

Photographs (following page 88)

The white sand of Port Olry's sheltered beach

St. Peter's Star, an Alia catamaran belonging to Jackers Fishing Company, moored in Lolowai Bay, Ambae

PREFACE

I plunged into *Deep Water* at the Australian National University in April 1986. As a visiting research Fellow in the Research School of Pacific Studies, I was fortunate to be able to write this book in an intellectual setting that both pampers and stimulates. I am grateful to the department's chairman, Roger Keesing, for accepting me and my husband as visiting Fellows. Keesing and the rest of the department made us feel welcome, and they provided an environment full of challenging questions, warmth, and wit, which made writing this book a pleasure.

While in Australia, I presented part of Chapter 8 as a seminar called "Loaves and Fishes: Problems of Development in a Catholic Community in Vanuatu" to the Department of Anthropology at the Research School of Pacific Studies. I gave an earlier draft of Chapter 10 as a seminar in the Anthropology Department at the University of Sydney. Excerpts from various parts of the book are included in my 1987 article in the *American Ethnologist*.

The Social Sciences and Humanities Research Council of Canada provided funding for the project; in particular, I appreciate the Council's willingness to support me as a private scholar. Similarly, I am grateful to the anthropology departments at both McMaster University and the University of Waterloo for allowing me to maintain affiliations with them as a research associate.

A portion of the research for this book was done while I was a consultant with the Canadian volunteer organization CUSO, and that portion was presented in my 1986 report. Some of this research I include here as the Appendix. I would like to note that I am not an employee of CUSO and that *Deep Water* does not represent CUSO officially or unofficially. I alone am responsible for any errors of fact or interpretation in this book. I wish, however, to express my gratitude to the many people in CUSO who facilitated the study: Garry Bargh,

Raymond Clark, Sydne Rich, Frances Tanner, the cooperants whom I interviewed in Vanuatu, and the returned volunteers who spoke with me in Canada. I am especially grateful to Gerald LeGal for assisting with the research in Santo and for his diplomacy.

To the people of Longana and Port Olry who cooperated with this study, I owe a debt of gratitude for providing much of the information that made this book possible. I extend special thanks to Edison Mala, Pere Sacco, Leah and Alexandre Samsen, Petro Rite, Pascaline Teguebu, and Boniface Tsintsianous.

The Fisheries Department of the Vanuatu Government generously provided information and office space; in particular, I would like to express my thanks to Richard Kaltonga and Richard Stevens.

I am grateful to the National Planning and Statistics Office for assistance and especially for allowing me to keep my computer in their offices. ORSTOM, the French research organization, and especially Gilbert David, made available a wealth of data on fishing in Vanuatu for which I am most appreciative.

In Canada, I am grateful to Matt Cooper and Dorothy Counts, who read the first draft and offered helpful suggestions regarding revisions. Vicky Fawcett made constructive editorial comments on the Introduction. I also appreciate the help of students in Anthropology 2100 (winter 1987) at York University whose reviews of the manuscript helped me to revise the book for readers like themselves. Kellie Masterson at Westview Press sustained me with her enthusiasm for the project. Finally, I want to thank Bill, Sean, and Channing for their unceasing support during the research and writing of this book.

I have changed the names of the volunteers and islanders with whom I worked to preserve their anonymity. Furthermore, I have altered identifying details concerning people's families and places of origin, and I have sought in every way to comply with the standards of ethics for research conducted under the auspices of the Social Sciences and Humanities Council of Canada.

Margaret Critchlow Rodman

1

INTRODUCTION

At times, in the hot stillness of early morning, there is no horizon in Vanuatu. Gray sky blends with sea. Dark islands seem to float on their own reflections. Only the shallow waters closest to shore glow aquamarine where the tropical reef gives off blues not reflected in the sky. On a rhythmic swell of waves the dark outline of a fisherman rises and falls, suspended between sea and sky, his outrigger canoe almost invisible. The fisherman's floating silhouette alone marks where the sky and the lagoon converge to meet the deep water.

Like the sky and the lagoon, a variety of forces and people converge in the introduction of deep water fishing to villagers in the Melanesian archipelago of Vanuatu (ex-New Hebrides). The lone canoe fisherman is the focus of this program to introduce small-scale, simple technology commercial fishing in the rural areas; as such, he—or, in rare instances, she—receives the attention of fisheries department officers, volunteers from half a dozen western nations, aid donors from Europe, Australia, New Zealand, Canada, and Japan, businessmen experienced in fish marketing, and FAO experts, among others. The possibility of catching 100 kg of premium quality red snapper in a day, with a market value of at least $US 100 is now an option available to the fisherman who equips a small craft with an outboard motor and a couple of handreels, and drops his line in water 100 to 400 m deep on the islands' reef slopes. For many islanders, small scale commercial fishing offers an attractive opportunity for earning money where coconuts previously provided the major—and in some places the only—source of a cash income. Yet, morning and evening, solitary canoes still mark the hazy horizons of Vanuatu fishing for consumption, not for sale.

Like a canoe poised far above the sea bottom where the Pacific

Ocean meets the reef slope, the people of Vanuatu are at the confluence of two environments—their own and the world of outsiders. Like the reef, this meeting point is not new; it is an ever-changing product of a particular past, and, in a small way, of global forces. The water is deep where the fishermen of Vanuatu grapple with a world beyond that has come ashore, and, unlike the clarity of the sea in Vanuatu, this deep water often is murky.

Why Vanuatu?

One purpose of this book is to take readers on a journey that will allow them to see development issues from the vantage point of Vanuatu. It seems safe to say that Vanuatu is beyond the periphery of most North Americans' geographical knowledge, although it is the center of the world to the islanders living there. The islands are probably best known through James Michener's *Tales of the South Pacific*, and through articles in *National Geographic* on the land-divers of Pentecost Island or on one of the world's most accessible volcanoes on the island of Tanna. The country's name is unfamiliar even to most anthropologists. And some of those who know that it used to be the Anglo-French colony of the New Hebrides still have trouble pronouncing the name the islands assumed at independence, "Vanuatu"—the trick is to enunciate every single letter and put the accent on the second "a."

The islands of Vanuatu form a roughly Y-shaped chain 1,300 km long in the lower lefthand sector of maps of the Pacific, lying between 13.5° and 22° south of the equator. The Solomon Islands are northwest of Vanuatu, and the long island of New Caledonia's Grande Terre flanks the group to the southwest. The Fiji Islands lie across an open expanse of sea to the east.

Vanuatu consists officially of "some 80 islands"; it is hard to be more precise because what constitutes an island is not always clear.[1] Many of the islands in Vanuatu are tiny; for example, the island of Rowa has only 10 ha. of dry land. The two largest islands (Santo and Malekula) make up almost half of the surface area of the group.

The people of Vanuatu have been known since the country achieved independence in 1980 as ni-Vanuatu. In the last census, which was in 1979, Melanesians comprised 94 percent of the population of 111,251 residents. The ni-Vanuatu population is estimated to be growing at a rate of more than 3 percent per annum, so the country's population probably numbered about 128,000 by 1984.[2]

Why is it important to know much about such a tiny country in the South Pacific? One reason is that the newly independent Pacific island states, of which Vanuatu is one, have the potential to exert a political and economic influence out of proportion to their small land areas and populations. Any understanding of the islands today must begin with the sheer immensity of the sea in which they are set. The Pacific Ocean covers about 165,384,000 sq km or more than one-third of the earth's entire surface. All the dry land on earth could fit into the area occupied by the Pacific Ocean. There are some 30,000 islands in the Pacific, ranging in size from tiny coral atolls to Papua New Guinea, which is the second largest island in the world.[3]

When I was a child, I liked to spin the globe that stood on a table in the corner of our living room. I would close my eyes and lightly hold my forefinger against the spinning globe, and wherever my finger came to rest I would consider visiting, at least in my imagination. I always hoped the spin would not end, as it often did, with my finger in the Pacific. The ocean didn't count as a destination; it was just a lot of blue that was nobody's country. That is no longer the case. Spinners of today's globes will find that the map of the New Pacific is not a fine spattering of islands in an expanse of blue. Now that island countries claim 200 mile Exclusive Economic Zones, the map of the Pacific is a continuous grid of national territories that extends from the east coast of Australia all the way to Pitcairn Island.

Missionaries have competed for the souls of islanders since the nineteenth century, but in the late twentieth century the grid of little countries with large territorial waters has been the focus for a new kind of evangelism.[4] Competition for economic and political influence between Japan and Russia is especially evident in Vanuatu where a recent fishing agreement giving Russian vessels landing rights in Vanuatu has spurred Japan to expand its economic assistance in the region.[5]

So far, Vanuatu has played a renegade's role in foreign policy. In 1982, Vanuatu's minister of foreign affairs refused landing rights to an American naval vessel paying a courtesy call because the ship, in keeping with longstanding US policy, would not declare if it was carrying nuclear weapons. This set the stage for New Zealand's subsequent, strong anti-nuclear stance. In 1983, Vanuatu became the first nuclear free nation in the Pacific, banning, in advance, nuclear power plants as well as the dumping of nuclear waste. The members of the South Pacific Forum, which represents independent states in the region, signed a treaty in 1984 banning nuclear testing and dumping, but not visiting warships. In other words, Vanuatu's anti-nuclear stance, while consistent with other island Pacific countries, went farther.

Non-alignment, including refusal to seek diplomatic relations with either the US or the USSR, was consistent with this anti-nuclear

4

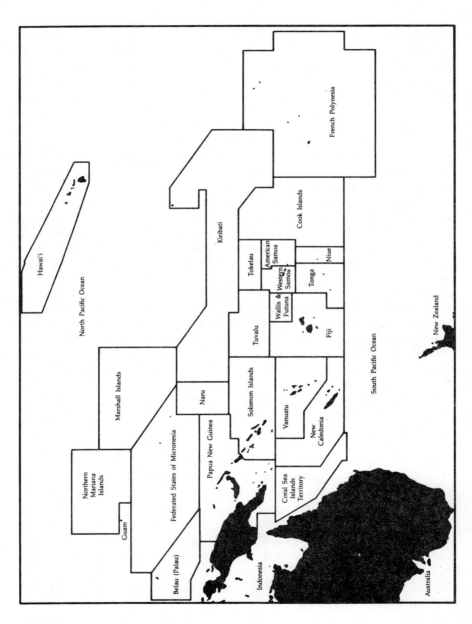

MAP 1
The New Pacific

policy. But more recently, Vanuatu's intrepid independence in dealing with powerful nations has worried New Zealand and Australia. It is one of the first South Pacific "micro-states" (after Kiribati) to have negotiated a fishing deal with Russia. More disturbing still to other countries in the region is the fact that Vanuatu is the only Pacific island country to have established diplomatic ties with Libya, Cuba, and the Soviet Union.

Development for Whom?

Given the power both of Vanuatu's new allies and those, such as Australia, that find the tiny country's foreign policy deeply disturbing, Vanuatu's claim to seek "self-reliance" seems politically compromised. The goal of achieving self-reliance by 1990 was central to the new republic's first national development plan. But self-reliance is not only politically problematic, it is economically elusive. The country's imports far exceed exports in the monocrop economy based on some of the worst quality copra (dried coconut) in the world. If self-reliance means increasing productivity to the point where exports equal imports in value, then Vanuatu has a long way to go to achieve this level of development. Fisheries development can help achieve this goal if local fish can be substituted for their imported equivalents; but increased productivity in the commercial sector may weaken the ability of islanders who fish for subsistence to feed their families. If these villagers reach the point where they have to go fishing in order to earn a wage instead of going fishing in order to catch supper, they may be less self-reliant as a result of "development."

One of the most basic questions that remains unanswered concerns whether the resource exists in quantities sufficient for sustainable development. In other words, are there enough fish in the waters of Vanuatu to support a variety of both commercial and subsistence fisheries? Ongoing research will provide answers to this question, but plans to develop the fisheries also are proceeding apace before the answers are ready.

Other questions need to be asked in order to evaluate the extent to which the fisheries development program is helping to achieve the goal of self-reliance. Are attempts to increase productivity in the rural sector realistic? Are they really likely to increase productivity in the long run or are increases in productivity bound to be temporary? Will fresh fish replace imported tinned fish in local diets? What will happen to income earned from participation in the fishing program?

In the simplest terms, what difference will the Village Fisheries Development Program make to villagers, to the volunteers involved in the program, to the state in Vanuatu, and to the aid donors who are funding the development projects? A shared goal of self-reliance holds different, even contradictory, meanings for each of these participants in fisheries development.

Self-reliance, like so many other commonsensical concepts, means very different things to people who think they agree on the meaning of the term. In Vanuatu, "self-reliance" (in all three official languages—English, French, and Bislama) is a widely understood concept with a range of meanings. In the views of planners and other agents of the state, progress toward the long-term objective of achieving self-reliance requires expanding and strengthening the economic base.[6] This involves economic growth, namely an increased productive capacity flowing from the use of larger amounts of land, labor, and capital, and/or the more efficient use of these resources. But more than economic growth is at stake. The concern is also with development, meaning the improved social and economic well-being of people throughout the islands. Development in Vanuatu emphasizes smoothing out regional and rural-urban disparities. Ultimately, the goal is to generate enough local revenue to pay for government services in each of eleven local government areas. For islanders, development does not just mean elected representatives, smoother roads, and better schools; it also means paying the price for these benefits in the form of taxes, licensing fees, and school tuitions. Generation of export income and domestic revenue in Vanuatu means persuading villagers to engage in more productive activity. In other words, the objective is to get more rural people working full time to earn more cash regularly from exportable commodities like copra and fish, and to spend the money they earn on locally produced items, local investment, and local services in the public and private sectors.

Self-reliance has a different meaning for villagers than it does at the state level. For rural islanders, self-reliance no longer means providing for their own subsistence without recourse to money. Those days are gone. And self-reliance never meant depending on oneself or one's immediate kin for social and economic support. Islanders were always part of broader local and family groups. Extensive trading in pigs, ceremonial valuables, and food linked the islands long before the colonial era. But self-reliance does mean keeping one's options open. Working full time at any one activity would curtail certain options. A village household needs to allocate its labor to alternate ends: for example, to ceremonial and other social obligations that ensure social security and social reproduction; to gardening for subsistence; and to other activities such as copra production and fishing that generate cash. Islanders continue to hedge their bets in dealings with the capitalist marketplace. Basically, almost no one in rural Vanuatu is willing to be a full-time anything.[7]

Rural islanders' views of self-reliance and those of the cooperants working for the Canadian volunteer organization, CUSO, are not the same, although both are different from the kind of self-reliance to which the state aspires. The idea that small is beautiful is most popular among people who have experienced the hi-tech, consumer-oriented way of life with which small and simple are contrasted. Islanders, in my experience, have no objection to acquiring the things that money can buy. What they resist is being forced into the position where *all* they have is what they can buy. None of them is reduced to this position in any absolute sense; but the ni-Vanuatu are well aware of some of the perils of commercialization, even if the ones that worry them are not always those of consumerism and the profligate use of natural resources that concern the volunteers.

These three contrasting views of self-reliance highlight contradictions between state planners based in one of the country's few urban centers, small producers in the rural islands, and the volunteers in between. The contradiction between these views is evident in the fact that if most village fishermen were expected to produce for export, self-reliance for the country measured in export dollars would mean a loss of self-reliance in the rural areas where the objective is to maintain one's social and economic options. The different views seldom come into conflict. In fact those who hold one view rarely express an awareness that the other views exist. Yet the contradictions are crucial for understanding the dynamic in which, to some extent, islanders' lives are constrained by the development project. In other ways they are making the new fishing activities fit into their ongoing way of life.

A persistent problem discussed in literature on development theory concerns the extent to which a way of life such as the simple commodity economy of the islanders of Vanuatu can be independent of the capitalist economy which operates at and beyond the state level.[8] A recent argument holds that such people can remain "uncaptured" by the state indefinitely, although effective development, in this view, will require their being drawn fully into the capitalist economy, whether by carrot or by stick.[9] How independent can such people be from the larger economy? How do people participate in capitalist markets without eventually adopting a capitalist mode of production?[10] How does the larger economy articulate with local modes of production, which may be categorized as tribal, peasant, or simple commodity economies? Can development occur that does not require fuller incorporation of simple commodity producers into a capitalist economy? And what are the consequences, both positive and negative, of "capturing" and transforming such ways of life?

Questions concerning the self-reliance of peasants and tribal peoples remain unresolved, partly because more attention has been paid to theorizing this issue than to ethnographic analysis of the factors interacting in particular cases.

This book offers such a case study. When I was a graduate student, I had a professor who often asked what a case study was a case *of*; it ought to be a *case of something*, like measles or theft or gingerale. So what is this study a case of? It is a case study that differs from others in describing a development program that is neither a dramatic success story nor a dismal failure; in some ways, it has been a moderate success and in other ways something of a failure, depending on how one looks at it and on who is looking. The viewpoints and voices in this book are multiple because there is no single, simple reality. And the case, like real life, is complex.

As we shall see, islanders participate in capitalist markets, especially through sales of cash crops. Some work for wages. Some seek new sources of income through development projects such as the one described in this book. Some make a little copra from their coconut trees when they need cash; others make copra regularly, earning thousands of dollars a year. Some save their money in Barclay's Bank; some take out loans to buy fishing boats; some buy Polaroid cameras; a few spend most of their small cash incomes on Fosters lager.

While participation in the cash economy through markets is part of everyday life for islanders, relatively few are, or want to be, more deeply involved. The tie between producers and the means of production is not easily severed in the islands. Landlessness is a cultural anathema. Customary land tenure is enshrined in the constitution, meaning that, at least ideally, no islander can be without access to residential and garden land. By and large, workers retain control over where, when, and how to expend their energies. They don't have to work full time to earn the money that they need so long as they maintain their gardens and keep up social relations with neighbors and kinfolk.[11]

The Vanuatu case is unique, but it raises questions with broader implications: To what extent do people involved peripherally in a market economy make a virtue of their marginality and seek to keep their distance from a capitalist mode of production? Under what conditions and to what extent do they succeed? Such questions, and the sketching of answers offered in the chapters that follow, reflect a deepening concern in anthropology with what it means to say that the kind of people we have traditionally studied often have greeted externally imposed changes with resistance, not passive acquiescence.

By resistance I do not mean to conjure up an image of naked warriors, their arrows tipped with poison attacking a commercial fishing boat as it enters the lagoon. Indeed the only crowds that gather at the sight of a fishing boat are potential consumers, not of the crew but of its catch. Resistance need not imply violence. The interaction between different forms of production in Vanuatu has created, and continues to create a particular history in which islanders and their cultural systems both constrain and are constrained by world capitalism. Working for money has not led to the demise of other forms of production, nor have capitalist modes of exchange replaced customary ones.

Fishermen around the world are known to be independent-minded, and the fishermen of Vanuatu are no exception. This book explores how they are responding in cultural, political, and economic terms to the commercialization of fishing on a small scale. It examines their relations with a state that, for reasons to be explored here, is both unwilling and unable to make capitalist development more constraining in the rural areas. Mainly, the islanders' independence speaks of their power and of their cultural resilience in the face of more than a century of contact with forces of development.

Notes

1. The source used for this round figure is "Vanuatu in Figures," a pamphlet put out by the National Planning and Statistics Office (Vanuatu 1984c). The 1958 Geneva Convention defined an island as "a naturally formed area of land (however small) surrounded by water which is above water at high tide" (cited in Gopalakrishnan 1984:8); this definition would apply to hundreds of islands, some very small indeed, mostly within a few hundred meters of another larger island. Another reason for the vagueness about the precise number of islands relates to Vanuatu's claim to the tiny Matthew and Hunter islands, which is contested with New Caledonia.

2. Population data come from the preliminary report on the 1979 national census (Vanuatu 1983) and from Haberkorn (1985).

3. David Stanley's *South Pacific Handbook* (1986), from which these facts are taken, is an excellent guidebook for readers who are planning—or wish they could plan—to travel in the region.

4. "Strangers in Paradise," a radio series prepared by the Australian Broadcasting Co (1981), makes this point very well.

5. References to increased Japanese aid in response to increased Russian influence in Vanuatu include *The Far Eastern Economic Review* 1986 (134(40):26).

6. The meaning of self-reliance in the State's ideology is summarized in the

first national development plan (Vanuatu 1982:10) and in the mid-term review of that plan (Vanuatu 1984:16).

7. I am indebted to CUSO cooperant Jerry Fitzpatrick for this succinct expression of the episodic participation characteristic of simple commodity production in Vanuatu.

8. The fundamental unit in simple commodity production is the household. This is a domestic economy in which the producer directly determines how long and how hard to work (Chayanov 1966:42; see also Sahlins 1972 on the domestic mode of production, and Durrenberger 1984 for examples of how anthropologists have developed Chayanov's ideas on the equilibrium of family demand satisfaction and the drudgery of labor). Generally, simple or petty commodity production emerges as a consequence of association with capitalism. This does not mean that simple commodity producers **are** capitalists or potential capitalists; in fact there is increasing evidence that simple commodity production, and peasantries more generally, can persist indefinitely in the face of capitalism. In other words, simple commodity production is not necessarily a transitional form on the way to becoming a capitalist mode of production.

Simple commodity forms seem never to have been dominant and tend to be found in association with capitalism as the dominant mode of production (see LeBrun and Gerry 1975, and Harriet Friedmann 1980). For a recent theoretical discussion in conjunction with a case study of forms of simple commodity production among West African canoe fishermen see Emile Vercruijsse (1984). Carol Smith (1984a, 1984b) has developed our understanding of the cultural as well as material characteristics that particular forms of simple commodity production assume, building (in 1984b) on Chevalier's (1982) illustration of Bourdieu's (1977) thesis that cultural as well as material contexts constrain social practice within constantly shifting power relationships.

9. See Goran Hyden (1980, 1983). For a critique of Hyden's position see Kasfir (1986).

10. See Eric Wolf's distinction between capitalist markets and capitalist modes of production in *Europe and the People Without History* (1982:297-298). Basically, this distinction is as follows: rational economic enterprise based on an expectation of profit and on the employment of existing wealth to gain future wealth can take place in capitalist *markets* that exist outside the capitalist *mode*. For example, the operation of a world market in copra is necessary for the emergence and reproduction of simple commodity production in Vanuatu, but the principles that govern capitalist relations of production need not be brought into play in order to participate in that market.

11. In Melanesia, politics traditionally has had a strongly materialist base. At times, the acquisition and distribution of wealth has seemed to outsiders to exhibit a capitalist logic (Keesing 1976, Strathern 1975). Like other analogies with Western experience, this one has been debated (see Connell 1982). Ultimately, the importance of consumption is tied to the need for social insurance that neither one's own production nor the state in Vanuatu can

provide, but that can be ensured through sharing what one has and fulfilling customary social obligations. This leads to the empirical question of just how the simple commodity economy reproduces itself, a question with which Joel Kahn (1980) has dealt in a structural analysis of the petty commodity economy of Minangkabau peasants; he concludes that there the system strains against increases in productivity, against the accumulation of surpluses, and against social inequality.

2

FIELDWORK

A week before Christmas in 1969, I awoke in my upper berth on the third-class deck of the French steamer, *Caledonien*, knowing that our journey from Sydney had ended. The ship was dead in the water in the breathless heat of dawn. A loading boom rumbled somewhere above my head. Chunks of copra, the size of potato chips and the texture of tire rubber, sifted through the open porthole onto my bunk. I remember being surprised that dried coconut smelled so little like food.

I was following my husband to what anthropologists call The Field. Bill was embarking on research for his Ph.D. in anthropology; I was along for the adventure. Our destination was the capital city, Port Vila, in the islands that are now Vanuatu, but were then the Anglo-French Condominium of the New Hebrides. The trip had taken ten days, during which time we had come to know our shipmates over meals aromatic with garlic, Gauloise cigarets, and Algerian red wine which had a thick rusty sediment from its 44 gal drum "cask." We shared a table with a Presbyterian missionary family bound for the backsliding island of Tanna, a middle-aged couple who had quit their jobs in Australia to drop out Sixties-style and travel the world, and a North Vietnamese father returning home with his sons to Port Vila where he worked for Shell Oil.

We did not plan to stay long in Port Vila. We disdained the civilized amenities of French and British colonialism; the plain truth was that we could ill afford the expense of life in the capital. We planned to find a village that was remote, but not too remote, on the northern island of Ambae—which was then called Aoba or, occasionally, Lepers' Island—and spend at least a year conducting research.

Bill found the kind of village he was looking for in the Longana district on the southeast coast of Ambae. We settled into three tiny rooms in a resthouse in Navonda village, about an hour's walk from the Anglican mission at Lolowai Bay. We stayed there for 14 months. At first we were helpless, unable to speak either the pidgin known as Bislama or the local language. Our neighbors laughed at us and helped us; we grew to be friends and even family.

We slowed our pace to the rhythms of island life. Our days were punctuated with sounds at first exotic, that soon became routine. Our alarm clock was a World War II shell casing that served as a gong calling villagers to worship at the Anglican church. Only a handful of the most devout actually went to morning and evening prayers, but everyone went to church on Sunday. We became accustomed to the roosters who crowed at all hours of the day and night, to flying foxes who squabbled in squeaks like a child's party favor as they fed in the fruit trees at night, and to the persistent snuffle of pet pigs who so loved to be scratched between the ears that they would crumple to the ground, weak in the knees with pleasure.

On my first day in the village, I sat with a contented sigh on the beach under a swaying palm; ahh, paradise, I thought. Immediately, I was startled to see a woman running toward me, crouched like a soldier under fire. She pointed to the ripe coconuts poised ready to fall on my head. Not speaking the language, I couldn't have understood her if she had added that the anthropologist seemed to have less intelligence than a two-year-old child, but I quickly learned that smart people look up before they sit down. After a while, I never even heard the intermittent thud of ripe coconuts plummeting 20 m to the ground so long as I was out of range. But I have yet to lose the reflex everyone develops living in a grove of palms. Even in Canada, I still jump aside if I hear a sound like the rustle a coconut overhead makes as it breaks free and heads for the ground.

On weekdays, the buzz of a light plane no louder than an outboard motor caught everyone's attention. The daily flight from Santo to the grassy airfield about 1 km from Navonda usually arrived sometime between 10 am and 2 pm. During our first fieldtrip, the sound of the plane was a signal with the force of Pavlov's bell. It meant lunchtime. Islanders know that the concept of three meals a day is a western one that has become part of their own way of life through a history of working on whitemen's plantations, mission stations, and the like. So perhaps it was appropriate that an emblem of western technology, the airplane, should signal a meal, bad jokes about the cannibal past aside.

But the meaning of the sound of planes has changed. On our later fieldtrips, our neighbors laughed about people who dropped everything at the sound of the plane and began to eat. Such people had come to be seen as local yokels because they had neither watches nor the cultural sophistication to know that it was silly to eat lunch at 10 am. Similarly, by 1985, schoolchildren no longer hooted with excitement at the sound of an approaching truck or jumped out of classroom windows to get a better view of the passing vehicle. Babies had ceased to howl in terror when they saw me, associating any white woman's face with the Australian nurses who gave DPT injections. The changing sounds of village life reflect the growth of a casual familiarity with development. Nurses are now ni-Vanuatu, trucks are commonplace, and the plane is just a plane not a dinner bell.

In 1970, the focus of Bill's research was on a traditional, customary activity. He analyzed the graded society, a system of ranks through which people (primarily men) rise by killing and exchanging tusked boars and intersex pigs. We attended dozens of rank-taking ceremonies and grew used to the chilling, almost human cry of pigs dying. After the killing, we enjoyed staying up all night and "dancing daylight." We joined moonlit circles of dancers moving slowly to the rhythm of slit gongs, which are hollowed-out logs of various sizes beaten with sticks. And we learned to pound our bare feet on the reverberating, volcanic earth in counterpoint to the drums, while a feast of pork that would be ready at dawn cooked slowly in pits filled with hot lava rocks.

We worked our way through the puzzles of the graded society. I drew elaborate maps of ceremonial settings and charts in three colors to document the bonds of kinship connecting participants. Bill interviewed old men who had reached the highest ranks, youngsters who were just entering the system, and occupants of every grade in between. We learned that high rank signifies personal achievement; it is not a matter of ascription. Even the sons of high ranking men have to make their own way in the graded society once they have passed beyond the childhood ranks. Nor does high rank ensure that a man will be a political success; to be a leader, one has to hold high rank, but not all high ranking men are leaders. The graded society has an intricate structure. Five major ranks that involve the killing of tusked pigs alternate with those in which pigs are exchanged between the rank taker, his supporters, and his sponsor. The alternating rank structure is illustrated in Figure 1.

Local languages have a wealth of words to describe pigs. In addition to male and female animals, there are intersex pigs that possess elements of both male and female genitalia (although most look female to the untrained eye) and grow tusks as if they were boars. In

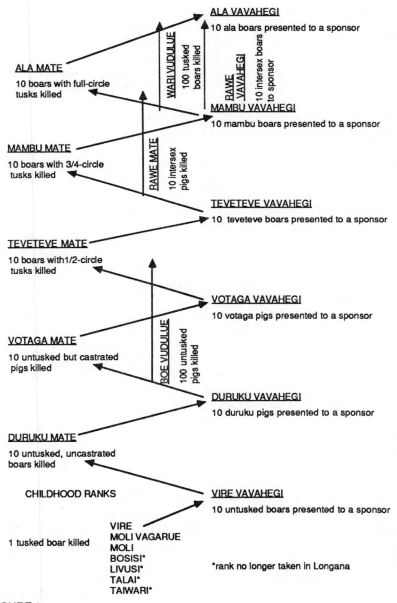

ALA VAVAHEGI
10 ala boars presented to a sponsor

ALA MATE
10 boars with full-circle tusks killed

WARIVUDULUE
100 tusked boars killed

RAWE VAVAHEGI
10 intersex boars to sponsor

MAMBU VAVAHEGI
10 mambu boars presented to a sponsor

MAMBU MATE
10 boars with 3/4-circle tusks killed

RAWE MATE
10 intersex pigs killed

TEVETEVE VAVAHEGI
10 teveteve boars presented to a sponsor

TEVETEVE MATE
10 boars with 1/2-circle tusks killed

VOTAGA VAVAHEGI
10 votaga pigs presented to a sponsor

VOTAGA MATE
10 untusked but castrated pigs killed

BOE VUDULUE
100 untusked pigs killed

DURUKU VAVAHEGI
10 duruku pigs presented to a sponsor

DURUKU MATE
10 untusked, uncastrated boars killed

CHILDHOOD RANKS

VIRE VAVAHEGI
10 untusked boars presented to a sponsor

VIRE
MOLI VAGARUE
MOLI
BOSISI*
LIVUSI*
TALAI*
TAIWARI*

1 tusked boar killed

*rank no longer taken in Longana

FIGURE 1
Structure of the Graded Society

order for boars and intersex pigs to produce large tusks, islanders remove piglets' upper canine teeth; this operation allows the lower canine to grow without abrasion or obstruction. Each stage of tusk development has a name, from the tiniest tooth called "a grain of rice" to the full-circle *ala* tusk. In fact, there are many named varieties of full-circle tusks to indicate, for instance, whether the tooth forms a circle outside the skin of the mouth or whether the tusk is large relative to the body size of the animal.

Rank-taking begins in childhood. A father tries to give each of his sons and daughters a tusked pig to kill. Such a gift shows love and respect for his children; it is part of bringing them up properly. Girls usually take rank only once more, on the eve of their wedding in a ceremony intended to provide pork for the wedding guests as well as to augment the bride's prestige.

Boys who choose to go farther in the graded society are not on their own, by any means, but they do have to participate as adults, achieving rank in their own right. Once a young man passes beyond the childhood ranks he must broaden his network of supporters, no longer depending on his father alone for pigs.

Exchange is fundamental to graded society activity, as it is generally to life in Vanuatu. A rank-taker must have seven pigs of his own with tusk development appropriate to the grade he wants to assume; but he cannot kill those pigs in order to take rank. Instead, he must use them to buy woven armbands and other emblems of rank or to pay those who render such services as playing slit-gongs at the ceremony. For the pigs he will kill, he must rely on donations from people to whom he has contributed pigs on other occasions. The rumble of a slit-gong echoing through the hills in the weeks leading up to the ceremony, has reminded those who owe the rank-taker pigs that the time is coming to repay their debt. They must do so with interest, or else suffer embarrassment. For example, the gift of a boar with half-circle tusks killed two years ago must be repaid with an animal whose tusks form three-quarters of a circle.

On the day of the ceremony, the rank-taker waits humbly for supporters to bring the animals on whom the ceremony's success depends. He must not seem arrogant, so he would never wear his Sunday best; instead, dressed in a worn tee-shirt and shorts, no shoes on his feet, he waits quietly for the pigs to arrive.

In other words, a rank-taker's personal success depends on the will of others to help him succeed as he has helped them in the past and will help him again in the future. The understanding of this interplay between rank and equivalence, between individual and collective accomplishment that we gained on our first fieldtrip was important later when I began to study development issues in Vanuatu. Village fisheries development projects, for example, are new, but islanders respond to these projects with know-how gained in other areas of their lives. They apply attitudes toward wealth and success expressed through the graded society to new situations. Humility combined with organizational skill, a mastery of exchange networks, personal achievement, but not at others' expense: all of these qualities found in graded society activity are crucial both to the persistence of development projects and to islanders' evaluations of whether such projects are successful.

We have returned to Longana three times since that first fieldtrip. Exploring the significance of the graded society at Bill's side had given me a deep curiosity to know more anthropology. I went to graduate school and in 1978–79, we spent 11 months in Longana while I conducted my Ph.D. dissertation research on the consequences of customary land tenure for cash-cropping coconuts. I returned to Vanuatu with my family for 5 months in 1982 on a postdoctoral fellowship to study consumer behavior. Our most recent fieldtrip was from July to December 1985 when I conducted the research for this book while Bill pursued his interest in a longterm study of legal change in the islands.

After our initial research in Navonda, we had a bamboo house built in a hill village known as Waileni, meaning "a different wind." We chose the village because some of our closest friends in Longana lived there. Also, the nights were cooler in the hills, too cool for mosquitoes and good for sleeping. Since the building of our house in 1978, Longana has become a second home where we go to be with friends and family, some of whom we have known since birth as Longanans have known our two children.

A local carpenter built us a thatched kitchen and covered the floor with white coral trucked up from the coast. Whenever possible, islanders prefer to have kitchens that are detached from the houses in which people sleep; reasons for this include keeping rats at a distance from one's bed, and minimizing the loss of life and property where there is no fire department. The carpenter equipped the separate "sleeping house" with an iron roof and a gutter on one side leading to a 200 gal tank, our sole source of water. The interior is really one room, about 5 m by 7 m, with partitions to mark off two sleeping areas for ourselves and our children at the back. The house stands on low stilts; the springy bamboo floor bounces like a trampoline when one of the frequent small earthquakes hits, and even when a puppy lying in the doorway scratches a flea.

Sense of place and the idea of rootedness are very important to the people of Vanuatu.[1] As soon as we had our own house, we ceased to be visitors in the same sense we had been in Navonda. Although we had stayed there for fourteen months, we had seemed to be passing through. We had camped out in the rest house, sharing our quarters with the occasional British or French colonial official on a tour of the district. Although the rest house was a solid, cement structure, our relatively flimsy bamboo house gave us far greater permanence in the community. In Navonda, we paid rent—the house was theirs; in Waileni we paid for the construction of the house—it was ours. We would come and go between Waileni and Canada, but our return would always be expected, just as local people expect their relatives who work in Vila to return to their Longana homes for vacations from time to time.

We assumed a place in the local scheme of things. We liked the fact that a visitor to Waileni could not instantly identify our house as the anthropologists'. With a corrugated iron roof to catch rainwater, it is fancier than some in the village, which have only thatched roofs; but it is a modest dwelling in comparison to those of our neighbours with cement walls and floors.

Our house stands on land belonging to Bill's adoptive father, a leader in the graded society. Sons in Longana usually live on their father's land; they follow a practice of virilocal residence, meaning that wives move to their husband's homes at marriage. Since both partners in most marriages are Longanans, a bride who moves to her husband's home does not leave her own kin far behind; she may not even leave her natal village. Nevertheless, there are crosscurrents of loyalties in the social structure of any settlement, many of which arise from the combination of virilocal residence with matrilineal descent. In Longana, as in some other parts of Vanuatu including Port Olry, everyone belongs to the same descent category as their mothers. Women transmit membership in this category to their children; men do not. Two major descent categories, or moieties, exist in Longana; people also belong to subcategories, or clans, within each moiety. The moieties, although matrilineal, are named after two men of mythic renown, called Tagaro and Merambuto.

Neither moieties nor clans are landholding units, but moieties are crucial to the formation of groups who orchestrate ceremonial activity. A rank-taker must ask a member of his own moiety to perform certain services at his graded society ceremony; other tasks must be done by a person from the opposite moiety. At weddings, the two moieties weave elaborate patterns of exchange traced with the passage of woven pandanus mats. The moiety to which the bride belongs gives certain mats to the groom's moiety and vice versa. The groom's gift of mats, along with pigs and other valuables, must slightly exceed the bride's family's offering.

The complexity of bridewealth exchanges comes in layers like the Western wedding cakes that are now an added part of Longana nuptial rites. Relatives by birth, or kin, perform roles that alternate with relatives by marriage, or affines. Different generations also play their parts. The bride and groom belong to opposite moieties, but the bride's mother and the groom's father share moiety affiliation as do the groom's mother and the bride's father. The groom's brothers will have married women of the same moiety as his bride; unmarried sisters of the bride will use the wedding celebration as an opportunity to flirt with likely young men in the groom's moiety. The children of married sisters belong to the same moiety as the bride herself, but her brother's children do not.

In practice, the working out of the binary principle of moiety affiliation creates entangled webs of kinship guaranteed to baffle not only first year anthropology students but also fieldworkers like myself. How does one ever sort out who's who at a wedding? How does anyone know what to call an old woman from the other end of the district whom one has never seen before? I asked such questions persistently during my first fieldtrip.

In Vanuatu, men always sit with men and women with women. This is true in church, in casual get togethers, and at traditional ceremonies. At weddings, I would sit with the women in the shade at the edge of the ceremonial ground. No one ever sat directly on the grass; to do so was considered unhealthy. In our culture we may catch our death of cold by standing in the rain; there, standing in the warm rain was okay, but sitting on the ground was believed to make one susceptible to colds. So we sat on the colorful, 2 m lengths of cotton cloth each woman used for carrying children, keeping the sun off her face, smothering giggles, and swatting flies.

The pace of events was always desultory; I developed a tolerance for hanging around in the fly-blown heat of noon. Often, the women around me slumped to the ground and dozed. But not me. I would remind myself that my adoptive affiliation was Merambuto moiety. That much I knew. I had even figured out that Longanan kinship followed a bifurcate merging terminology, such that the sex of the relative through which a person is linked to others is crucial; in other words, a mother's sister is called by the same term as a mother while a father's sister is called something else. What I had not managed to do was to put this principle to work in labelling the people in my environment. How I was related to the other wedding guests? I was at a loss as soon as I tried to trace links beyond my most immediate kin.

I was especially unsure of myself when I contributed mats as wedding presents. A group of Merambuto women would spring to their feet, ready to file into the thick of things and present the mats piled on their heads. I would jump up to join them, only to feel someone tug at my dress, laugh and say, "Sit down! Those are the bride's *mothers*. You're her *sister!*"

On my second fieldtrip, the simplicity of the system became apparent, not because I was older and wiser but because we had by that time had a child. Longanans took pains to ensure that our six-year-old son would not be as socially inept as I was. He soon learned to listen to his mother—not me, but my adoptive sister who is therefore his Longanan mother. If she called someone father, in the local language, Sean called him grandfather. If she called him son, then Sean knew to call him brother. Sean also listened to his adoptive father. He learned not to blink when his father greeted a child "Hello, Brother;" Sean knew enough to call the little kid his own age "father." I recognized this skewing pattern, such that a father's sister's sons are called "fathers," as one that is characteristic of Crow type terminologies; but little Sean was the one who knew what to call the kid.

So if Sean were at a wedding in Longana ten years from now he would know how to address other guests he had never seen before. He would simply work outwards from the people to whom he already knows how he is related, listening to the terms they use for the strangers and labelling them accordingly. He could even call people from other islands by appropriate kinship terms. For example, equivalents to the Longana moieties are found in Port Olry, so all he would need was one Port Olry resident to whom he could trace a kin or affinal relationship in order to find his place in the community.

I have included examples of a few of our Longana fieldwork experiences not only to give the flavor of the place and the people, but also to indicate the importance of ties based on exchange, rank, kinship, marriage and residence. I have not even introduced the politics of the place, the land disputes, the factions, accusations and oratory that mark a leader's waxing and waning influence. All of these ties are expressed through places as well as people. They not only draw together people and places; they separate them, making each person and each locale a distinctive intersection.

An understanding of such ties is important to this book because neither development workers nor participants in development projects exist in isolation from their societies. Often the development workers must build their houses on the social and geographical periphery. The fisheries adviser's house may be at a mission station, or on the far edge of a village, or at a location on the coast that is good for fishing but not a residential center. This may be unavoidable. But if the program is to succeed, the development worker will be woven into the fabric of social life, in somewhat the same way as we were.

The people who come forward to participate in development projects are not isolated individuals. To be an isolated individual in Vanuatu is to be an outcast, which is extremely rare. Participants in development projects are the tip of a social iceberg. They share their involvement, their success, or their failure with others. Their participation is a matter that involves others in their community, others in the intersecting circles of their kin and affines, and others in the networks of exchange that politically and economically empower them as individuals in a social world.

Researching Fisheries Development
in Port Olry

For five months in 1985, I studied the social consequences of village fisheries development in Vanuatu. Part of the research was academic, funded by a Canadian research grant, and part was performed as a consultant for CUSO, the Canadian volunteer organization. My time was divided three ways: First, I conducted research at the Fisheries Department in Port Vila and Luganville (pop. 5621) on the large northern island of Espiritu Santo. Then I spent six weeks in the village of Port Olry on the east coast of Espiritu Santo where one of the largest Village Fisheries Development Projects is in operation, consisting of 15 independent fishing boats and a fish buying association with a coldroom. Finally, I spent the rest of the time in Longana, the district on the southeast coast of Ambae where my husband and I had worked on three previous occasions since 1969. The VFDP fishing project in Longana was based at the mission and government headquarters at Lolowai Bay. The project was very small, consisting of just one 8-m Alia catamaran fishing boat. CUSO volunteers had been associated with both the Port Olry and Longana projects during the preceding two years, but the volunteers had returned to Canada by the time I arrived.

It was hard to conduct research in Port Olry. Not only were villagers generally reluctant to trust any outsiders, especially whites, the manager of the fishing association felt he had little to gain from my presence. Although he seems to have discounted the significance of the research at first, later it became quite clear that he feared my study might endanger his position.

Manuel, the Port Olry man who was manager of the fishing association as well as village chief, had agreed to my study in principle, and the Fisheries Department had sent a representative to the village several times to make arrangements for my visit. As a consultant working for CUSO but with close ties to the Fisheries Department, my terms of reference were to assess the social consequences of Remre Fishing Association for the village of Port Olry. In particular I was to identify the degree to which Remre had achieved the objectives of the Village Fisheries Development Program, which are:

1. to promote the development of small-scale fishing,
2. to provide employment in the community,
3. to decrease urban drift,
4. to improve nutrition,
5. to reduce dependence on tinned fish and meat, and
6. to provide cash for local development efforts.

My impression was that Manuel at first paid little attention to me because I was a woman. In general, I found being anomalous facilitated my work in Port Olry. People were not sure what to make of me as a woman, a white, a fluent Bislama speaker, a person deeply familiar with a culture similar to but not quite the same as Port Olry. Fishermen in Port Olry found me less intimidating than they would have found a white man. In contrast to their expectations of white men, I could listen to and make note of their opinions without imposing my own ideas. Still, as Manuel made a point of telling me the moment I met him, a ni-Vanuatu researcher would have been better. I agreed and explained that CUSO had arranged for a Papua New Guinean to conduct the study of Remre's social impact on the community, but these plans had fallen through at the last minute, no ni-Vanuatu with the right qualifications could be found, and I was recruited because I had planned in any case to be studying fisheries development in Longana on Ambae Island, whose silhouette is just barely visible from the Port Olry beach.

Following this exchange, I interacted with Manuel daily as I went about my work in Port Olry with my ni-Vanuatu research assistant, Pascaline. Manuel made no attempt to impede my work, and he was willing to show me all his record books once he had time to go over them himself first. He laughed about the fact that some people were suspicious of my study, but promised that he would let me speak at the next village meeting, whenever one might be held, to explain my presence. He was particularly amused when one of the major shareholders in the fishing association refused to speak to me. For me, the incident was distressing because it made me feel as if, somehow, I did not exist. I wrote in my journal:

Roughest part of the morning was when, on Celia's brother's recommendation, I went to talk to H. who is a boat owner and known to be a good fisherman. He was sitting on the beach with R. and several younger men. I gave my usual explanation of my work—in fact I thought it was a better than average performance. H. just sat there, staring out to sea, pretending I wasn't there. I hung around, becoming increasingly uncomfortable, and finally asked Pascaline if she could find out what the trouble was. She said, "He doesn't want to talk" which was all too obvious by then. I suggested to H. that we'd be going now and I would be happy to hear from him anytime he wanted to talk.

After the episode on the beach, I spoke to Manuel, saying that I wanted to know when he could hold a meeting so that I could try to gain people's cooperation. The next two Sundays were out of the question, he explained, because of a political rally and a wedding celebration, and no one would come to a week-night meeting. "Oh well," Manuel concluded, "If no one will talk to you and you don't get far with your study this time, you can come back some other time." "No I can't!" I responded heatedly, and Manuel just smiled.

After a week in Port Olry, Pascaline and I were continuing to find a few people each day who would agree to talk with me about fishing. It seemed to me that Manuel was disappointed that I had not given up and left the village. He always greeted me with a smile, but his joking manner had assumed a sinister tone; "I'm getting tired of white faces in this village," he said to me. "Maybe I'll run you out of here!"

Although my work was proceeding, ten days into the study it was slow going. One morning, I was walking with Pascaline through the village with a clipboard tucked under my arm on which to write notes about household fishing activity. At each house Pascaline would explain that I was trying to find out about how often people fished, what techniques they used, and so on; I would explain that I was doing the study for CUSO to find out if Remre had changed certain aspects of life in the village and what the local people thought of any changes that had occurred; then Pascaline would ask if someone in the household would be kind enough to speak with me for a few minutes, and explain that the information I gathered would be confidential. She gave this spiel in Tolomako and Sakao languages; I gave it in Bislama.

This particular morning neither of us was having much success. It was discouraging to watch a man duck into the back entrance of his house and then to be told by his wife at the front door that she was so sorry but her husband wasn't home right now. We walked dejectedly along the sandy street wondering if we should do something else with the rest of our day. We passed a plump, middle-aged woman pinning her washing on the line. She called to Pascaline. "You know why people are afraid to talk to Margaret?" she asked. We stopped and the woman explained to Pascaline that villagers feared we were writing down information that would be used to impose a tax on fishing boats, fishing gear, or even on the fish themselves. The source of the rumor, she said, was Chief Manuel himself.

Fear of taxation runs deep in Vanuatu. It would have been easy for Manuel to build on local resistance to the government, sowing seeds of yet another rumor of impending taxation, this time a tax on fish.

I tried to put a stop to the rumor. Thanking the woman who was pinning her laundry on the line, Pascaline and I turned and strode back down the sandy street. We stood in the glare of the morning sun and I called out to those in the houses where no one would speak to us. "Do you think I'm here to tax you?" I shouted. "Why, yes, we do!" came a gruff voice from behind a bamboo wall. A tall, heavy-set old man with a flowing white beard hobbled over the threshold. The three of us moved into the shade of a mango tree and spent the next hour talking. He began to relax. "You mean you're not going to tax every wave that comes ashore?" he joked, and then he began to tell me about his household's fishing activity.

This marked a turning point in my study. Although I could never say that I felt welcome in the village as a whole, I did feel welcome in many households. Some people went out of their way to be helpful, bringing gifts of fresh vegetables as well as offering information. And some of those most strongly antagonistic to Manuel were also willing to spend hours with me, to ensure that I gathered their opinions of Remre Fishing Association and fisheries development in general.

In five weeks in Port Olry, Pascaline and I were able to conduct research at the four major stores in the village and at three of the remaining six small stores. We gathered information for a detailed review of Remre's financial situation. I assessed the economic viability of commercial fishing and compared fishing with copra as a way for villagers to earn cash incomes. We undertook a survey of household fishing activity and an enumeration of the resident population using observation and local knowledge to supplement what people were willing to tell us. We conducted a census of household construction. With the help of Gerald LeGal, a CUSO cooperant in Luganville, income from copra, cocoa, cattle, and fish sales were identified from buyers records for 150 households in the Port Olry area. Ultimately, I conducted interviews with representatives of about 50 households. Topics ranged from the history of the settlement, through fishing experience, to villagers evaluations of the fishing association and suggestions for the future.

Notes

1. See Joel Bonnemaison (1986), Margaret Jolly (1982) and my own work on place in Vanuatu (1985a, 1985b, 1987b).

3

FISHING FOR FOOD

Deep water is a resource that Vanuatu has in abundance. To be precise, its territorial waters span 680,000 sq km of sea.[1] In contrast, the land area of the archipelago is small—less than 14,000 sq km. The abundance of deep water, however, does not mean an abundance of fishing grounds. The islands generally are volcanic and corraline in origin. They rise precipitously from the sea bed and are skirted in most cases by skimpy fringes of reef. In some places, such as the Canal de Segonde in Santo, the land drops away so sharply that huge container ships carrying supplies from Australia glide past, a mere stone's throw away from women collecting shellfish in water up to their knees. Only 1.5 percent of Vanuatu's territorial waters are less than 400 meters deep. If the reef shallows are excluded, just 7,547 sq km remain to make up the zone between 100 and 400 m in depth that is suitable for deepwater handlining. This is the activity that is the focus of the Village Fisheries Development Program, and of this book.

Although the area suitable to deep water handlining is relatively small, the activity's importance to the country's development could be considerable. Snappers and other deep water fish potentially could provide good sources of protein in the otherwise rather low protein diets of islanders. Slash and burn, or swidden, cultivation of yams or taro is the basis of the rural economy. Beef, chicken and reef fish are treats. While it is common to purchase some foods, such as tinned fish and rice, gardens remain crucial for most households. Cash-cropping, especially coconuts, has removed land from subsistence production and, especially in areas with high population density, people face a shortage of garden land. Yet the need for cash is increasing along with the need for more locally produced food. Village fisheries development offers a way of earning money that may encourage islanders to remain in the rural areas while enriching local diets and, overall, improving in some small ways the quality of life in the islands.

This chapter begins with a discussion of the geographical setting and population of Vanuatu, then moves on to describe traditional fishing activities. A key metaphor—that of a fish trap—is introduced as a way of understanding what I call the Melanesian success model. Most of the chapter then analyzes the diet of rural islanders, indicating the increasing importance of purchased items but also emphasizing that new things to eat are integrated into a customary system of foods.

Geographical Setting and Population

The first village in which my husband and I lived in Vanuatu was on the sea coast exposed to the tradewinds. This sounded idyllic to me, especially in the breathless humidity of February when any hint of a breeze was welcome and rare. But the tradewinds that began in May and blew until October were not what I had expected: they are a steady, roaring, pounding blast at about 40 km per hour from the southeast that leaves one speechless on the beach at the futility of trying to shout over the surf and the wind. The trade winds which indeed may have speeded trade across the Pacific in the days of sailing ships, can make trading difficult these days. Canoes and other small craft stay away from windward coasts in Vanuatu for half the year; even larger ships collecting copra in the islands avoid the hazards of standing off a lee shore when the tradewinds blow. Fishing in small boats is possible only where the islands themselves cast shadows of shelter from the prevailing winds and the accompanying south-easterly swells. See Map 2.

While the average population density in Vanuatu as a whole is only 11 persons per sq km, and only about half of the potentially arable land is in use, the population (128,000) is unevenly distributed and some areas are already experiencing pressure on land resources. The government is concerned to limit migration to the two urban centers, Port Vila and Luganville, and to make a rural way of life attractive to ni-Vanuatu now and in the future.

The population of Port Vila, which is the capital, was only 1,300 in 1955. In the aftermath of a cyclone that demolished most of the town in 1959, the shifting of business activity to Vila with the closing of Norfolk Island as a tax haven, and the development of tourism, the population of Vila had grown to 10,600 people by 1979. The January

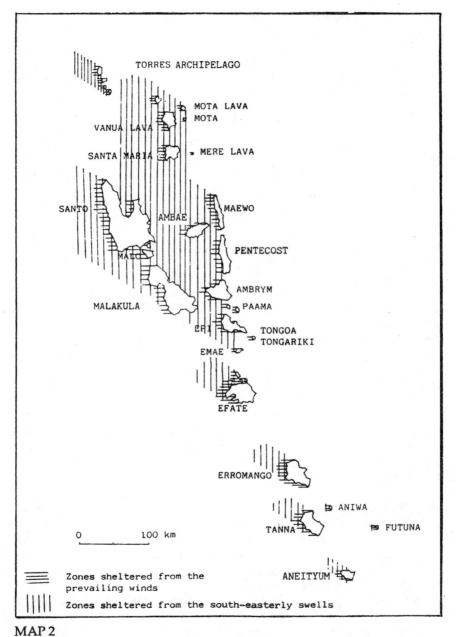

MAP 2
The Vanuatu Archipelago Fishing Zones in Relation to Swells and Prevailing Winds

1986 urban census found that Port Vila includes an estimated 14,184 inhabitants and has grown at a rate of 4.2 percent over the past five years.[2] Luganville, situated along the Canal de Segonde on the northern island of Santo, had experienced substantially less growth due in part to people avoiding (or being asked to leave) the area during the rebellion that occurred around the time of independence; from a total of 1,500 residents in 1959, Luganville had achieved an estimated population of 5,000 in 1984. So far, Port Vila and Luganville are the only towns in the country where the total population exceeds 1,000 residents.

Some of the smallest islands in Vanuatu have the greatest population density. On Tongoa island in central Vanuatu there are 900 people per sq km and on Atchin, a small island off the coast of the much larger Malekula, an incredible 1,870 people are crowded onto each sq km of land. Although the people of Vanuatu have traditionally been oriented toward the land as the source of the bulk of their subsistence, in islands such as Tongoa the sea is becoming an increasingly attractive resource. Fisheries development in these areas is directed toward making small-scale, commercial fishing using simple technology attractive to local people, providing them with opportunities to earn cash and to eat well without moving to town.

Fishing for Consumption

Fisheries Department programs have introduced islanders to new fishing *techniques*, but only in rare instances have they introduced islanders to *fishing*. There is no doubt that ni-Vanuatu have placed great importance on their land, and so on the production of both food and money from the land, but this does not mean that they turned their backs on the sea and its resources. The conviction that ni-Vanuatu are oriented toward gardening rather than fishing may be partly in the eye of the beholder. Administrators seem to be at least as traditionally "landminded" as the ni-Vanuatu are said to be; data on the length of paved roads and numbers of cattle have been easier to come by than information on maritime resources in many island states, and in Vanuatu, as is often the case, fisheries is grouped with land-based activities in the Ministry of Agriculture, Forestry and Fisheries.[3]

Notably, it was a recent *agricultural* census that revealed the ongoing importance of fishing as a productive activity in Vanuatu. In 1983, the Fisheries Department requested that questions on the socio-economic aspects of village fishing activity be included as part of the major agricultural census program. Fishing had always been seen as a pastime that contributes only marginally to consumption in rural

Vanuatu, but the results of the survey showed that this was far from the truth. Fishing, the survey concluded, is a widespread and popular activity in which about half the rural households of Vanuatu participate.[4]

Spears, bows and arrows, traps made of bush vines, and poison leaves all were part of what might be called traditional fishing tackle. Today, the spear remains important equipment, constituting 21 percent of all fishing gear. The bow and arrow is still used in some areas and accounts for 5.5 percent of fishing equipment in the villages. Traps, poison leaves and other traditional techniques account all together for only 1.5 percent of existing equipment, although a few old men remember how to use these ways of catching fish even in islands where they are no longer practiced.

For example, in the Longana district of Ambae fish traps retain cultural importance as metaphors, although only one old man can remember how to make them and he is too old to put his knowledge into practice.[5] The fish-trap metaphor is central to understanding the nature of "success" as a concept in Vanuatu; it seems worth exploring at this point because it is central to evaluating the extent to which fisheries development projects are a success in local terms.

A spherical trap of woven bush vines was baited with coconut and placed in the sea, held in place by stones wedged around the trap. Once in place, the trap might catch fish. In other words, the trap had the potential to become a container, enclosing objects of value (in consumption or exchange) and incidentally concealing them from view within the basketry beneath the surface of the sea.

Today, a successful person—a leader, a man who earns high rank by killing tusked pigs, a businessperson—is said to have a trap full of fish. Longanans say that the fish, like the followers of renowned men, are eager to find a way into the container, but once inside the trap they cannot escape. The metaphor of the trap connotes a cornucopia of wealth that is not obvious to the bystander, a resource that is not exactly hidden from view but that is not flaunted either, a wherewithal that is greater than it seems when viewed from the surface of things. Other people can only admire such a person. They can see *how* he does it, but feel they could not do it themselves. In essence, such a man is more than he seems; for he seems, at first, like any other man. But his success lies in his resourcefulness which is submerged, unnoticed by others until the moments when he achieves a goal that no one suspected he was capable of achieving. He buys a truck, holds a feast, or wins an election; and people say, "Who would have thought that man could do this! He has caught a lot of fish in his trap yet we never saw them." In other words, he is a success because he is more than he appears. Conversely, the most spectacular failures are those men who seem much bigger than they really are, those who inflate their personal abilities and achievements, who promise more than they can produce, and whose inner resources are a big, empty trap.

The survey of village fishing activity found that most rural islanders prefer to purchase their gear rather than use traditional fishing equipment. Overall, purchased fishing line comprises half of the fishing gear used in the villages. Spear guns (10 percent) and gill nets (4 percent) are also popular. Most fishing is still done on foot— from the shore, walking along the exposed reef, or standing in the shallows. Canoes predominate as fishing vessels when fishermen do go out on the water. Of almost 4,000 boats estimated to be used for fishing in the villages of Vanuatu, 87 percent were canoes of the traditional outrigger design.

The picturesque coastal village of Port Olry in Santo was my home for six weeks during the research for this book. I would go down to the beach late every afternoon with our two children and my research assistant. My five-year-old daughter swam while my assistant and I passed the time pleasantly, watching the fishing activity that often was at its peak toward sunset. Our son, aged 13, sometimes swam with his sister but more often watched *near* but not *with* us women. Adult men and teenage boys went out fishing in the village's many canoes using lines and nets; some cast their nets while standing in the water near the shore; those who had wanted to catch deep water fish to sell were well beyond the horizon in their outboard motor boats. Meanwhile, small boys took to the low branches of trees or perched on rocks along the shoreline and hurled improvised spears at the brightly colored fish in the shallows. Girls and boys below about the age of ten mixed together gleefully hunting schools of sardines where the river met the sea, and herding the tiny fish into the shallows. Once they had their quarry cornered, the boys used their hands and the girls took advantage of their sodden skirts to fling sardines by the dozens onto the bank.

Even children can afford to acquire the simplest purchased fishing gear. Our son, Sean, enjoyed watching other boys who fished every day after school from an old cement pier, and before long he decided to join them. For less than $US 1 Sean was able to equip himself with fishing gear that was identical to that used by the other boys on the pier. He bought 10 m of nylon monofilament line and two small hooks (one was a spare). With some coaching from my research assistant, who although female and thus in Port Olry a non-fisherperson, knew perfectly well how these things were done, Sean wound the line around an empty plastic cooking oil bottle. He tied the hook to the line; a carefully selected piece of coral, of a dull beige hue guaranteed not to make a fish wary, served as a sinker. The coral had a natural hole through the middle, making it easy to attach to the line. Like the other boys, Sean first cast his line with a bare hook—the idea being to fool some tiny fish into becoming the afternoon's bait—but the technique was considerably harder to master than it seemed from the apparently effortless success of the Port Olry boys.

Every day, variations of the scene we watched in Port Olry as the sun went down are played out in villages throughout Vanuatu. Approximately two-thirds of the seafood in the rural areas comes from inside the reef; the density of fishermen exploiting this resource is 18 per sq km, 80 times greater than the number of fishermen who utilize the 100–400 m deep water zones on the reef slopes.

Consumption of Fresh Fish

Fish, fresh or tinned, is a popular item in the Vanuatu diet. According to a recent French study, the total annual ni-Vanuatu production of fish and shellfish comes to an estimated 2,403 tonnes.[6] Most of this total is for home consumption; only 23 percent (555 tonnes) of the total catch was sold in 1983, earning an estimated $US 1,470,000.[7] Two-thirds of these fish and shellfish are found within the reef where a large variety of seafood is relatively easy to catch, compared to the effort—and expense, if a motorboat is involved—required to fish outside the reef where the variety of fish is much less and where there are few shellfish.

My research in Port Olry indicated that households ate fresh fish at about three evening meals a week. Ample supplies of fish were part of the diet, and this had been the case long before the introduction of fisheries development schemes; all but a few families could get fish whenever they wished—the exceptions being households headed by women in which there happened to be no boys old enough to fish effectively.

Some older residents of the village and some recent immigrants to Port Olry from the Santo bush eat no fish at all. These people follow a tabu or traditional prohibition on both eating fish and setting foot in the sea that was widely observed in the past. It was common for a specialist to attribute someone's illness to the consumption of fish or to entering the sea. Diagnoses through dreams often led specialists to prescribe that the patient never again eat fish or come into contact with the salt water.

On the Longana coast, the consumption of fresh fish from within the reef is low by comparison with Port Olry. Sea crabs or reef fish are sometimes featured at a feast, and a few households eat fresh fish often, especially those that include a young man who has time on his hands, access to a speargun, and enthusiasm for fishing. But in contrast to Port Olry, fresh fish is not commonplace in the Longana diet.

We do not know how important fresh fish is generally to the nutritional status of ni-Vanuatu, but a survey by a Canadian volunteer does give an indication of the place of fish in the diets of pregnant and nursing women. The diets of these women were felt to be very similar to those of adult ni-Vanuatu women generally, so the results of the survey have been taken to apply to the female population over the age of 19 years as a whole. This study found that, overall, only 42 percent of the women had consumed any protein during the previous day. There was a noticeable difference between the eating habits of urban women, of whom only 10 percent had failed to eat any food containing protein, and rural women, of whom 47 percent had not eaten any protein.[8] In the rural areas, inland women seem to have a considerably lower protein intake (55 percent) than coastal women; in the center of the southern island of Tanna, 80 percent of the women said they had eaten no food containing protein on the day before the survey.

Of the women who had some protein intake, 33 percent had eaten fresh seafood. In town, fresh seafood made up less of the women's diets than tinned fish, while women living in rural coastal areas eat three times as much fresh seafood as they do tinned fish .

Prior to the introduction of small-scale commercial fishing, people who wanted to eat fish generally caught it themselves or obtained it from another household member. So it is not surprising that even in 1983, purchases of fresh fish accounted for only 2 percent of the estimated total of household budget allocations in rural areas. Nevertheless, people may be buying more fresh fish now than they did a few years ago. An earlier study found that all together, fresh fish, fresh meat, and tinned meat made up only 2 to 2.5 percent of the monthly household expenditure.[9]

There is no evidence that ni-Vanuatu are substituting fresh fish for the tinned product, although import substitution is one goal of fisheries development in the country. In 1984, almost 800,000 kg of tinned fish were imported into Vanuatu for home consumption, surpassing the value of 1981 tinned fish imports by 34 percent. This was disappointing to those who had viewed a drop in the volume of imported tinned fish over the preceeding two years as a sign that local fresh fish might be substituting for canned imports. Even if the volume of tinned fish were to drop in 1985, it seems unlikely that a shift away from tinned fish is taking place in comparison to a clearcut example of import substitution, in which margarine has gradually displaced butter in the islands: 7

times as much margarine was imported in 1984 as in 1981 while the value of butter imports dropped by 29 percent.[10]

Obviously, fresh fish that one catches for "free" (discounting, for the moment, the costs in time and money of production) are preferable on economic grounds to purchased tins of fish. People say that they prefer the taste of fresh fish to tinned fish, but a love of tinned fish seems to run deep. Consider the ode to tinned fish written by a ni-Vanuatu girl and featured on the June page of a high school calendar (see Figure 2).[11]

The convenience of simply opening a tin compares favorably to the time-consuming, messy task of cleaning and scaling fresh fish. Tinned fish is also popular because it comes in many varieties. It is common for a store in a rural area to stock half a dozen sizes and brands of tinned mackerel, as well as a few varieties of pilchards and sardines. Results of an unscientific poll that I conducted in Port Olry and Longana revealed a strong preference for tinned mackerel in tomato sauce.

The question of which is the better buy, fresh or tinned fish, if one cannot catch one's own fresh fish, is difficult to answer. Variation by brand in the amount and quality of fish in a tin, as well as variation in the nutritive composition and price of different species and cuts of fresh fish complicate attempts at comparison. Still, there is some evidence that tinned fish not only is cheaper but may also be better for you than the fresh fish we tend to assume is such healthy food. Tinned fish generally contains higher levels of niacin, riboflavin, iron, and calcium than fresh fish, because the bones are cooked in the canning process. The flesh of fresh fish contains twice as much water as tinned fish, but, on the other hand, water or oil may be added to tins of fish along with salt. Tinned fish contains almost twice as much fat as fresh fish. One study found that in 1984, 80 cents would buy 450 grams of tinned tuna in brine or 275 grams of fresh red snapper. The study concludes that tinned fish is nutritionally a better deal, because "just about everything" is edible in tinned fish (except, as the study fails to note, the tin itself), while only about half the purchased weight of a fresh fish can be eaten.[12]

In my view, the fresh product compares more favorably with the tinned than this study indicates. A 100 gram portion of fresh fish contains 104 calories and 19 grams of protein; the same amount of tinned fish has 188 calories and 20 grams of protein.[13] In the rural areas, 667 grams of snapper could be purchased for 80 cents, yielding 694 calories and 127 grams of protein. For the same amount of money, one could purchase 450 grams of tinned fish containing 840 calories and 90 grams of protein. In other words, an islander can buy more fresh fish for his or

Tin Fish

By CAROLYN KALORAN.

OH Tin fish what a lovely food. Everyday We eat you. When we eat you we always think Of the fish in the Sea. Every afternoon and dinner we eat you you are nice. When we finish eating you but still we want to eat you. OH what a lovely food you are.

June

	Mon	30	2	9	16	23
	Tue		3	10	17	24
	Wed		4	11	18	25
	Thu		5	12	19	26
	Fri		6	13	20	27
	Sat		7	14	21	28
	Sun	1	8	15	22	29

FIGURE 2
Ode to Tinned Fish from a High School Calendar

her money than tinned fish, and, although it has fewer calories, the fresh fish has a protein content similar to that of tinned fish.

But tinned fish is clearly a better buy than red snapper in town, where for 80 cents one can buy only 275 grams of the fresh product, yielding 286 calories and 52 grams of protein. With half of the urban ni-Vanuatu work force earning less than $160/month in 1983, tinned fish was more attractive than fresh fish, especially if snapper was the fresh fish of choice.[14] There are cheaper fish available in town. The price for mixed reef fish at the Port Vila fish market was the same as the butchers charged for the cheapest stewing cuts of beef in 1985 ($1.80/kg).

Other Purchased Foods

In any case, the amount of money households spend on fresh fish in the rural areas is trivial compared to the five items that comprise a hearty 46 percent of the average household budget, namely rice (22 percent), tinned fish (8 percent), bread (6 percent), sugar (5 percent), and soap (5 percent).[15] With one exception, these are all price-controlled items; and with the same exception, they are all imported goods. That exception is bread. Nowhere is the French colonial influence more delightfully apparent than in the quantity and quality of the local bread. Chinese bakeries in Santo and Port Vila produce crusty loaves daily by the thousands. These sell for 20 cents each, and sometimes it seems as if every man, woman and child in town eats a loaf a day. In the early morning, the smell of fresh bread fills Port Vila. Battered Toyota cars, crammed so full of bread that long baguettes stick out the windows, careen around the side streets in the cool, predawn darkness, honking at every turn to bring customers from their beds to buy bread. Almost every Air Melanesiae flight to the outer islands leaves Port Vila in the early morning with a rice bag full of hot bread among the cargo; at that hour, the little planes smell better than any airline I've ever flown, a delicious mixture of fresh bread combined with the scents of soap and baby powder as clean passengers set out on a journey from the capital.

In the outer islands such as Ambae, bread is more of a luxury than in town. Many villages have had free-standing cement bread ovens for years, constructed by the community to make bread for church celebrations or built by enterprising individuals; but these tend to develop cracks and fall into disrepair. Where there is no bread oven in working condition, someone often runs a small business making "gato namba 8," a doughnut-like deepfried cake (hence gato, from the French gateau) which sells for 10 or 20 cents.

While bread is popular, it is no substitute for the rice the ni-Vanuatu consume in even greater quantities. In 1984, Vanuatu imported 5,521 tonnes of rice for household consumption; the total value of imported rice was greater than the value of all the gasoline brought in to fuel the country's vehicles and generators. In other words, every ni-Vanuatu consumes about 43 kg of rice per year.

As is true of all cuisines, a system of foods makes up a meal in Vanuatu.[16] Traditionally, taro or yams were the staple items in islanders' diets, taro predominating among those who lived in the inland hills, and yams being grown by coastal peoples.[17] Food was covered with leaves and steamed in an earthen pit heated with red-hot stones. A favorite food that was made traditionally and continues to be very popular today is known in Bislama, the national language, as "laplap." Each language has names for many kinds of laplap, but in its basic form all laplap is made from a grated, raw starchy food—taro, yam, plantain or (these days) manioc or sweet potato. The laplap is wrapped in leaves and cooked among hot stones; before or after cooking, depending on the variety one is making, a topping of minced greens and/or coconut cream may be added. Such a creation is the centrepiece of a meal. But to transform laplap from a dish, so to speak,[18] into a meal one must add a garnish of fish or meat. Laplap without fish or meat is no more a meal than a hamburger without a bun at a barbeque; some people like it that way, but the host will try to find something, perhaps a piece of toast, to fill in for the missing bun. In Vanuatu, tinned meat or fish is acceptable as a substitute for fresh meat, which should be chicken or fresh fish with laplap. Recently, it has become popular to include an unopened tin of fish in a parcel of laplap given to visitors to take home with them.

This traditional system of elements in a meal is evident in the use of the newer foods, rice and tinned fish. Like taro or yams, rice is the main feature of the meal and is heaped in a pile that fills the container or plate in which it is served. The size of ni-Vanuatu portions of rice came as a surprise to us, and no doubt the first of our neighbors in the islands for whom we prepared a meal went away hungry for more rice. By the time we held our going away feast in 1982, we understood the system well enough to know that two 50 kg bags of rice would not be enough to feed the anticipated 200 guests, even though the meal also would include an entire steer. A third bag of rice and 100 taro ensured there would be enough food for everyone to have what our neighbours called a "heavy" portion of food to carry away from the gathering and eat, Melanesian style, among their own household groups. We also picked up a few tips on entertaining from our island friends. For example, if instead of distributing individual portions of cooked rice, we displayed the rice in large piles, one for each hamlet, it would look "heavier"; what's more we would use less rice.

Heaviness is something to which ni-Vanuatu cuisine aspires, rather the way that French baking aspires to lightness. To some extent, rice has come to provide the desired heaviness, as a substitute for starchy tubers, but taro or yams are still unsurpassed for adding a truly satisfying bulk. Like traditional laplap, rice must be garnished with a bit of meat, a chunk of fish, or, preferably, a mixture known in Bislama as "soupsoup" made of onions sauteed in cooking oil with a little curry powder, to which water and sometimes green vegetables are added along with the meat or fish. The origin of this meal dates back to the early days of contact between ni-Vanuatu and the white men who developed an interest in their islands and their labor during the 19th century.

There is a growing dependence on commercial purchases of food in Vanuatu, but this is a very gradual process. As historical roots of the "soupsoup" meal suggest, elements in the cuisine have changed slowly. This conservatism, ironically, favors change where fish is concerned. While snapper, as we have seen, may be no substitute for tinned fish, it can garnish a plate of rice as nicely, by local standards, as a chunk of beef or a leg of chicken. It fits into the system. Reef fish has, as it were, made a place for all other fresh fish atop a heap of rice. Whether the village fisheries development program will consistently yield fish to fill this place in local diets remains to be seen.

Notes

1. Offshore resources began to assume new importance in Vanuatu even before independence when the South Pacific Forum introduced 200-mile nautical zones in the region in 1976. The Law of the Sea Convention held in April 1982 by the 3rd United Nations Conference on the Law of the Sea further sanctioned 200-nautical mile exclusive economic zones for the South Pacific States, although the USA refused to sign this treaty (Bergin 1983:20-21; Asia Yearbook 1984:112). The data on Vanuatu's sea area come from Penelope Ridings (1983).

2. As reported in the national newspaper, *Tam Tam*, 22 March 1986.

3. See Couper (1986:1-2) and Emmerson (1983:2).

4. This corresponds to about 8,600 households. The information on this survey comes from Gilbert David's published report (1985) and his personal communications with me.

5. Contrary to David's (1985:5) claim that fish traps are not part of traditional fishing equipment in Vanuatu, having been introduced by recent Polynesian immigrants, the Longana people claim to have had fish and bird traps as part of their customary heritage.

6. Ibid.:6.

7. Sales of fish made up 42 percent (240 tonnes) of this total, but accounted for only 13 percent of the total value. Higher priced crayfish represented 45 percent of the total volume and 83 percent of sales value. Research conducted a year later suggested that overall fish production might be as much as two times greater than previously thought (David 1986:19–20). The variability may have been due to methodological differences between the two surveys.

8. Ming Hung (1983).

9. Terry McGee et al. (1980). These findings were based on a survey conducted in 1975 (cited in Cillaurren and David 1986:22).

10. The source for these figures is unpublished data provided through the courtesy of the National Planning and Statistics Office.

11. What I have labelled the ode to tinned fish appeared as part of a 1986 calendar prepared by the creative writing class of Lamenu Bay High School, Epi, Vanuatu in 1985. I am grateful to the class teacher, Vicki Poole, for permission to include this excerpt.

12. David (1986:25).

13. I am unable to determine the basis for the figures used in David's (1986) calculations. For my own analysis I have relied on the Table A.1.5 in the Liklik Buk (1986:234), a rural development handbook.

14. Quille (1985) cited in David (1986).

15. David (1986:22).

16. Mary Douglas's (1974) article "Taking the Biscuit . . ." on the structure of English meals is a clear, and amusing, illustration of the systematic structure of meals. See also Jean-Marc Philibert's work on consumption and systems of goods in Vanuatu (1986, 1988).

17. See Jardin and Crosnier (1975) and McGee, et al (1980) for further information on food consumption.

18. Of course, laplap has its own dish in the form of the leaves in which it cooks. Fresh green ones are used to serve portions of the laplap. I liked to think of the dark green stands of laplap leaves near settlements as an ecologically sound equivalent to a ready supply of paper plates.

4

DEVELOPING VANUATU

The Europeans' ships were probably the first thing that ni-Vanuatu noticed about the white men who visited their islands. In May 1606, three ships under the command of Pedro Fernandez de Quiros, a Portuguese explorer sailing under the Spanish flag, dropped anchor in Big Bay. Believing that the island he had found was in fact the elusive southern continent, Quiros named it "Terra Australis del Espiritu Santo," since shortened to Espiritu Santo, or even to just Santo. Quiros stayed 50 days in a vain attempt to establish a settlement, called New Jerusalem, as a base for missionary activity. When the Europeans interrupted a rank-taking ceremony, crossing a line drawn by the local chief to indicate how far the visitors could proceed, violence resulted. The death of one ni-Vanuatu, whose body was then hung from a tree prompted approximately 600 islanders to retaliate. The Europeans kidnapped several ni-Vanuatu males, stole pigs, and suffered from the climate, disease, and infections. Eventually, Quiros's men had had enough. They took the initiative and set sail from Big Bay while their captain was asleep. "The people of Big Bay were left with the memory of white-skinned men in strange clothes who travelled in floating villages, killed others in a mysterious way and stole pigs, boys, and food."[1]

On Ambae, there is a legend about a man who watched Captain Cook's ship sail past in 1774. Possibly, the ship he saw belonged not to Cook, but to another explorer, Louis Antoine de Bougainville. In 1768, a full 162 years after Quiros left Vanuatu, Bougainville sailed near the islands of Pentecost and Maevo, and landed at Ambae to take on wood and fresh water. The landing party was greeted by a volley of arrows, the islanders seemed covered with sores (which were probably yaws), and Bougainville chose to depart quickly, naming the place "Lepers' Island." Such a name may or may not have discouraged subsequent exploration; on a personal note, the name "Lepers' Island" did nothing to reassure my mother when I announced where in Melanesia we were going to do fieldwork.

In any event, by the time the legendary man on Ambae saw Cook's or Bougainville's ship, it is said that depopulation had already begun. In the story, the islander who watches the tall, white ship is alone, the sole survivor of a settlement wiped out by disease. Whether or not depopulation during that period can be linked to European exploration, and, as far as I know, such a link seems unlikely, the importance of the legendary account is that the mere sight of a white explorer's ship is so closely associated with a threat to the islanders' lives.

Before long, ships began to arrive in greater numbers, bringing white men who came ashore in search of more than food and water or the salvation of souls. At first, they came for sandalwood which was discovered to exist in commercial quantities on Tanna and Erromanga.[2] Sandalwood traders earned a reputation for ruthlessness that was not undeserved; but islanders did not simply stand by and acquiesce to the demands of the white visitors. From the outset, ni-Vanuatu were very selective about what they would accept in exchange for their wood, and they even raised the price of the wood to traders as supplies became short relative to demand. Traders found that they had to enter into agreements with islanders in order to get enough wood to make their business worthwhile; running roughshod over the native peoples might work once, but it was not in the traders' best interests in the long run.[3]

The first missionaries to Vanuatu, who followed on the heels of the sandalwood traders, were not welcomed. John Williams, his assistant, and three Samoan teachers from the London Missionary Society became martyrs on Erromanga within minutes after landing there in 1839. More Polynesian missionaries were sent to proselytize in the southern islands. The idea was that Polynesians would be more acceptable to the ni-Vanuatu than white missionaries; this hardly seems to have been the case, however, for the Polynesians suffered from the colder climate, fell sick with malaria, and found it difficult to communicate with the ni-Vanuatu because of basic differences between the Melanesian and Polynesian languages.[4] Both Polynesian and, later, European missionaries were believed to be sorcerers on occasions when epidemics broke out in the islands; some missionaries were killed and others fled for their lives. Nevertheless, the island of Aneityum was successfully missionized by the 1850s. During the second half of the nineteenth century, increasing missionary activity on the part of the

Anglicans, Presbyterians, and Roman Catholics brought Christianity to most of the islands.

Along with the missionaries and traders came new goods. Islanders at first sought such items as fishhooks and calico; later their interest in a variety of knives and other metal tools increased. Stick tobacco became popular and, because it was quickly consumed, created a continuing demand, something that pleased the sandalwood traders. Towards the end of the trade in the 1860s, islanders began to acquire muskets and powder in exchange for sandalwood. New tools and such items as cooking pots and cloth changed the way of life in the islands, largely by reducing the amount of time spent on daily tasks. Some of the time made available in this way was devoted to warfare, which the new muskets made a more deadly activity. Those with access to the white men's goods had a new source of power, and part of that power consisted of increased knowledge of the world beyond the village.

The ships that brought the sandalwood traders and missionaries also carried curious ni-Vanuatu off to see the white man's world. Anglican missionaries brought young men from Vanuatu to New Zealand, and later to Norfolk Island, to attend college. In 1847, 65 ni-Vanuatu were recruited to work in Australia, the first of thousands of men from the archipelago to participate in what became known as the Labor Trade. Life on a grazier's plantation apparently did not suit the first contingent of young men who, clad only in their loin-cloth-like penis wrappers, "walked the 400 miles back to their manager's office in George St., Sydney—to the horror and consternation of Sydneysiders. To everyone's relief their manager booked their passage home as soon as possible."[5]

The sugar producing district of Queensland in northeast Australia was the destination for which most ni-Vanuatu laborers were recruited between the 1860s and the turn of the century, although islanders were also sent to work in Fiji, Samoa, and New Caledonia. The sugar industry needed a steady supply of cheap, docile labor, at least until the 1890s when a new system of sugar production, using smallholdings and central mills, was introduced. The abuses of recruiting ships, also known as "blackbirders," are well known and the inadequacy of attempts to regulate the trade helped to bring recruiting to an end.[6] In some instances, islanders were kidnapped and abused; but other men and, in smaller numbers, women signed on willingly. The reasons for going to Queensland often had to do with a desire for adventure and for the goods that were offered in payment for one's labor.

As in the days of the sandalwood trade, islanders quickly established the best terms of trade that they could. There were clear preferences concerning destinations as well as tradegoods. At times, the white men themselves became prizes in variants on traditional competitions for prestige. For example, Longanans attacked and killed the boat's crew of the recruiting vessel "Mystery" in 1878. The purpose of the attack seems to have been to increase the renown of the local leader who masterminded the raid. When there was virtually no reprisal for the killing, another Longanan chief looked to a white man's ship; he needed a victim on whom to vent his grief over the death of his son, and so killed and ate two crew members of the "May Queen," another labor recruiting ship. The British navy, however, did not let this attack pass unavenged, and sent a patrol ashore to traverse the island. The patrol shot one islander and burned a village, making it clear that killing members of a boat's crew was not always politically astute.[7]

The Colonial Period

In the late 1880s, Britain and France established a Joint Naval Commission in an attempt to keep some control over law and order in Vanuatu. Britain did so reluctantly, having sought to avoid involvement in the islands which seemed to have the potential to become nothing but a financial burden. France, on the other hand, saw the islands as a good place to settle convicts released after serving their sentences in New Caledonia. Furthermore, France felt that the archipelago had commercial potential as a colony. John Higginson, an Irish Anglophobe who became a French citizen, acquired vast tracts of land in Vanuatu in the 1880s. He bought some of the land from British settlers who had come to the islands to grow cotton during the boom associated with the American Civil War and who had since fallen on hard times. The rest of the land was "bush," uncleared jungle ceded by islanders who had no way of foreseeing the implications of the agreements they endorsed and who, in some cases, were not even the customary owners of the land in question.

Within a few years, Higginson's landholdings were assumed by the French government. French interest in the islands continued to grow, French settlers outnumbered British settlers 2 to 1 at the turn of the century, and France began to push more strongly for annexation of the archipelago. Sentiment in Australia ran strongly against French annexation, and Australia tried to put pressure on Britain to increase its presence in the islands. There was no effective mechanism for resolving the land disputes with the islanders that proliferated as French and British settlers attempted to clear and cultivate the land. There was no way to deal with offenses except those that required "acts of war" and so could be settled by naval intervention.

The Anglo-French Condominium of the New Hebrides arose out of efforts to resolve these issues. Formalized by the Protocol of 1914, the Condominium was a unique and very inefficient form of colonial rule. Under the Condominium, popularly mocked as the "Pandemonium," the New Hebrides was not technically a colony but a region of joint influence over which neither Britain nor France was sovereign. The archipelago was not partitioned; instead it was administered jointly by two nations with very different intentions for the islands' future. France continued to regard the Condominium as a temporary measure that would lead to French annexation, while Britain continued to do as little as possible and to maintain its presence largely because of Australian pressure. British and French nationals were interspersed, although in many instances they tried to minimize contact with each other and some areas, such as Luganville on Santo, developed a distinctly French ambience. The differences in politics, culture, and language between the French and British were expressed in separate pockets of influence throughout the archipelago. These colonial differences also drove a wedge between groups of ni-Vanuatu who were already insular and divided by traditional animosities.

The dual government, or "Tufala gavman" as it was known in Bislama,[8] slowly gave rise to a Noah's ark of institutions: by the time the Condominium was dismantled in 1980, there were two police forces, two systems of health care, two legal systems, two jails, two school systems, two currencies, three official languages (French, English, and Bislama), two sets of district officers in the outer islands, two administrative headquarters in Port Vila, and two flagpoles carefully positioned so that the flag flying above the British Residency on an island in Port Vila's harbor was the same height as the tricolor that flew above the French residency on a hill above the town.

Yet amidst all this redundancy, the ni-Vanuatu, as neither French nor British nationals, were stateless and had legal protection only under a Native Code that often was haphazardly applied. Neither the French nor the British controlled the abuses of its citizens in the islands. The British police force was too weak and the French were more interested in encouraging settlement by French citizens than in punishing legal violations. For their part, the ni-Vanuatu continued to provide labor for plantations. The labor trade with Australia ended around the turn of the century, but recruiters within Vanuatu continued to enlist workers for local plantations in the islands. These plantations were mainly on the larger islands of Santo, Efate, and Malekula utilizing tracts of "dark bush," uninhabited land belonging to islanders but seldom if ever cultivated.

Ni-Vanuatu and Commodity Production

During the first half of the twentieth century, ni-Vanuatu became more and more deeply involved in the market economy, producing copra, selling their labor for periods of time, and forming their own small trading companies. Experience gained working on white men's plantations, along with encouragement from missionaries and traders, led ni-Vanuatu to start their own small coconut plantations on customary landholdings in the outer islands where large plantations had not been established. People planted coconuts in lowland gardens, so that once the food crop had been harvested, the coconuts could continue to grow in the abandoned garden. As more and more people followed this practice, moving from garden to garden year by year, and sometimes clearing larger tracts of land expressly for plantations, some areas of Vanuatu were given over entirely to coconuts. This was the case, for example, in Longana where a canopy of coconut palms rising from hundreds of smallholder plots came to cover the entire coastal plain.

Islanders sold their coconut meat to traders who lived locally or who dealt from ships. At first, raw coconut meat was strung like a flower lei on bushrope for sale, but ni-Vanuatu soon learned to smoke dry the coconut flesh, turning it into copra and earning a higher price for their product. By 1930, rural smallholders produced about one-sixth of all copra exported from the country (in 1982, they produced three-quarters of all copra exports). As their own plantations grew and islanders were able to gain the western goods they wanted through labor on their own plantations, they were less willing to work on white men's plantations except when the copra price was low; and, of course, when the copra price was low, white planters were reluctant to hire more labor. Ni-Vanuatu began to employ other islanders as plantation labor, especially on Ambae.[9] Some islanders started their own trading enterprises and prospered because they could live more cheaply than white traders and so undercut them.

Along with cash cropping, conversion to Christianity had a major impact on local ways of life. While some missionaries (notably Anglicans and Roman Catholics) had at least a minimal tolerance for such customary activities as pig-killings, exchanges of pandanus mats, and traditional dancing, others (especially the Presbyterians) flatly opposed such behavior as pagan. Until the 1950s, missions provided the only systems of health care and education in the islands. Thus it was in everyone's interest that the islanders continue to provide for their own social security according to custom, even if they were urged to abandon those aspects of customary behavior deemed to be at odds with their new Christian lives.

In other colonial situations, the state has intentionally "contained" traditional societies, preserving them to care for those who are too young, too old, or otherwise unfit to contribute their labor to the state. In Vanuatu, one can observe the same effect, for many traditional societies have survived intact, albeit transformed by the colonial experience. But in the case of the Condominium, it would be hard to see the preservation of customary ways and the maintenance of a sense of independence in many rural communities as an intentional policy of the state. For most of its history, the Condominium existed almost exclusively to hold a place for the potential national interests of Britain and France and to attempt, with little success, to deal with land disputes. The requirement that both resident commissioners had to agree on everything that was done, ensured that very little was accomplished and that everything took a great deal of time. The missions, while more efficient, had limited funds and manpower to provide social services. Both missionaries and planters discouraged at least some customary activities. But in many places, the islanders kept alive their customary systems of land tenure, reciprocity, ceremonial exchange, kinship and traditional medicine, and so could attend to their own well-being. This they did, even developing their own legal systems in some islands, and maintaining a deep-rooted sense of their fundamental autonomy that shrugged off the rivalries of the "tufala gavman" as a white men's problem.[10]

World War II

The Second World War provided new work experiences for ni-Vanuatu. During World War II, Vanuatu became a major American supply, aviation, and hospital base for the fighting in the Solomon Islands. Santo was the scene of the largest influx of Americans—some 100,000 service men were stationed there—and ni-Vanuatu in Port Olry remember that sirens sounded and lights illuminated the night sky from near their village all the way to Luganville some 65 km away. A fighter plane even crash landed on a coral reef a few hundred meters offshore, and Port Olry villagers watched in amazement as two airmen climbed unhurt from the plane. The pilot, it is said, was only injured *after* disembarking when he cut his leg on the coral. And the wrecked fuselage of the plane remains on the Port Olry beach to this day, its metal polished by the sand that shifts on the tide.

About 10,000 ni-Vanuatu worked for the Americans during the war. The experience, it is safe to say, changed their lives. Never had they seen so many western goods, nor had they seen wealth disposed of as the Americans did, dumping millions of dollars worth of supplies and vehicles into the sea at the conclusion of the war. "New equipment was destroyed to protect American markets; whole camps and workshops were emptied, trucks dumping their loads at the water's edge where cranes hoisted them into the sea. Eventually truck drivers did not even bother to switch off their engines or unload but let the cranes grab the loaded, running trucks and drop them into the saltwater."[11] The Americans paid well and are remembered as having treated ni-Vanuatu workers with relaxed good humor. Many of the gifts that soldiers gave to islanders are still treasured. I saw complete sets of green fatigues, US Navy plates and silverware, cooking pots and blankets, banners, bombs and brass shell casings, all carefully stored in the bamboo and thatch houses in which people live in the hamlets of Ambae.

Post-War Development

The Americans built bridges, roads, and airstrips that are still in use today. This was the first taste that most ni-Vanuatu had of what development was all about, but the post-war period was an anticlimax. Today, the little Britten-Norman Islanders that fly to the outer islands use only a fraction of the old runway at one of Santo's three bomber airfields. The main street of Luganville seems designed for some other town; a barren corridor of a boulevard, it was built by the Americans to be wide enough for two tanks to pass each other. The town has never grown big enough to fit its street, and, like the tanks, development has largely either passed through or passed it by.

The development that passed through Santo has been associated with agriculture—cattle, copra, and to a lesser extent, coffee and cocoa grown on large expatriate plantations—and with tuna fishing. Although ni-Vanuatu provided labor for expatriate plantations, it was the occasional planter who got rich, not the laborers and so most of what wealth there was to be gained from plantations, which was often very little, passed through. The Japanese-owned South Pacific Fishing Company has operated out of Palekula near Luganville since 1957. Taiwanese vessels under contract to the company operate within and outside Vanuatu's 200 mile zone, catching mostly tuna. Ni-Vanuatu in small numbers have served on the fishing vessels, and the government earns some revenue from the company ($160,000 in 1983).

But both ni-Vanuatu and expatriate residents on Santo felt by the time of independence that development had bypassed the island. Although Vila had received somewhat more attention, very little had been done to encourage economic self-sufficiency anywhere in the country. Beginning in the 1950s, the Condominium attracted more and more colonial officers who had worked themselves out of their jobs in Africa as countries such as Tanzania became independent; efforts began to be made to improve education, healthcare, agriculture, and communication in the islands. For example, by 1970, all ni-Vanuatu children could receive a primary school education. But as pressure began to mount in the late 1970s for independence, all parties to the Condominium—British, French, and ni-Vanuatu—wondered how the islands could best be shaped into a cohesive, self-reliant state. The task has proved to be ongoing and remains the highest priority of the Vanuatu government more than five years after independence.

The Struggle for Independence

Vanuatu did not achieve independence without a struggle, not a big struggle by world standards, but one that was big enough to represent deep-rooted discontent with the Condominium and to leave a legacy of political fragmentation. Two strands of the conflict associated with independence are relevant to this book, because they deal with questions of autonomy as these were expressed in Longana and Port Olry; these are the emergence of the Vanuaaku Pati and the rise of the Nagriamel movement. There were, and are, other important parties and movements in the Vanuatu political equation, but allowing them to enter the discussion here will just add confusion to a narrative that the Vanuaaku Pati and Nagriamel make complicated enough.

The issue of land rights gave rise to both the Vanuaaku Pati, the ruling party which had some of its roots in Longana, and to Nagriamel, a movement that sparked a rebellion in Santo in the months before independence in mid-1980. Land disputes and the lack of clear title to property had led to the formation of the Condominium; the same kind of problems in a different era led to its dissolution. Prior to the 1950s, neither the two governments nor the private sector had exhibited much interest in developing the islands. For both islanders and expatriates, commercial production was largely confined to making copra. Although at one point the amount of land claimed by expatriate alienators exceeded the total land area of the archipelago,[12] most of it remained what the ni-Vanuatu called "dark bush." Uncleared and unfenced by the Europeans who thought they owned it, the dark bush continued to serve as a resource for ni-Vanuatu who made gardens, hunted, and sometimes settled there, and who also thought they owned it.

A number of factors combined to change this live-and-let-live pattern and begin the sudden development of the dark bush that both Nagriamel and the Vanuaaku Pati emerged to oppose. Planters were having increasing difficulty obtaining cheap labor in the islands, and the copra market was such that there was little profit to be made in cash cropping unless production costs could be kept very low; but the world demand for beef was at an all time high as western standards of living rose. Vanuatu is well-suited to beef cattle, as the current production of top-quality grass-fed beef attests.[13] So in the late 1950s, expatriate settlers began clearing large stands of dark bush on Santo and fencing the perimeters of their claims. Land speculation also grew to an extent unprecedented since the days of Higginson, and assumed a new guise. In the 1960s, an American named Eugene Peacock began acquiring large amounts of land, including plantations caught up in heated land disputes with the customary owners. Peacock subdivided and began selling the land with the idea of attracting Americans to settle in what he advertised to be unspoilt retirement/vacation paradises in the islands. At first he was strikingly successful, making $5,000,000 by 1971 from his Santo investments alone,[14] but in the end the scheme collapsed, leaving only sandy paths through scrubby undergrowth to trace the outlines of what were to have been the streets of lavish American subdivisions.

Both the British and French resident commissioners disliked the thought of Vanuatu becoming a suburb of Hawaii for Americans, but they did nothing to halt it. In the words of one British official writing in 1969:

> There seems little point in developing the New Hebrides for New Hebrideans when in ten years time there could be (stretching the point as far as it will go) 25,000 Americans living here. I suppose there would be lots of jobs for black servants.[15]

But the potential "black servants" did not take kindly to the Condominium's inertia.

Ni-Vanuatu resistance was Peacock's undoing. Throughout the entire colonial period, islanders had resisted European encroachment on their customary lands and insisted on establishing their own terms for dealing with outsiders. But clearing the dark bush for cattle and the rise of a new kind of land speculation prompted innovative, more extreme forms of resistance.

In the early 1960s, the Nagriamel movement began on Santo in opposition to the alienation of customary land. Nagriamel became the first movement to unify ni-Vanuatu. By 1971, when the Condominium at last legislated against property speculation only to have the legislation opposed by European settlers, a second strand of resistance had coalesced in the formation of the New Hebrides Cultural Association, which was to become the first political party in Vanuatu.

By the time independence was achieved, the leaders of both Nagriamel and the Vanuaaku Pati had had dealings with the United Nations, both had promised to lead their followers to freedom, and both had maintained a fundamental belief that ni-Vanuatu land was inalienable from its customary owners. Yet, as events in the 1970s were to make clear, the differences between Nagriamel and the Vanuaaku Pati were profound. These differences were the legacy of the Condominium, of the mistrust that traditionally separated island groups, and of outside influence in anticipation of independence. In 1980, these differences culminated for Nagriamel in rebellion and for the Vanuaaku Pati in the formation of the new country's first government.

Longana and the Vanuaaku Pati

The Vanuaaku Pati began as the New Hebrides Cultural Association at the time when we were conducting our first fieldwork in Longana in 1971. The association centered on young, English-educated, ni-Vanuatu working with the Anglican church in Santo and at Lolowai, headquarters for the Diocese of Melanesia in Vanuatu. In the early 1970s, the Lolowai community consisted of a hospital, a lepresorium, two boarding schools, and several churches set on green slopes like amphitheaters shaped by long-extinct volcanic spatter cones, one of which broke open to the sea forming a picturesque little bay. Longana land adjoins Lolowai. The harbor at Lolowai Bay provides the only good shelter for boats in the area and has been heavily used by Longanans over the years to ship their copra out and bring supplies in from Santo. So it was natural that Anglican Longanans, coming and going frequently to Lolowai, should be among the first supporters of the cultural association. Father Walter Lini, who was instrumental in founding the New Hebrides Cultural Association and went on to become the first Prime Minister, was Longana's parish priest at the time of our first fieldwork, which made local people—and us—particularly aware of the emergence of an unprecedented political consciousness. The Cultural Association staged the first demonstration ever held in Vanuatu; in 1971 its supporters took to the streets of Port Vila in response to the settlers' opposition to legislation that severely restricted land speculation. On Ambae, flag-raising ceremonies, barbeques held to raise funds, and even the casting of ballots were all as new for Anglican Longanans as demonstrations in the streets were for urban ni-Vanuatu.

Independence in 1980 ratified unswerving local faith in the party and deepened Anglican Longanans' conviction that the Vanuaaku Pati provided a pathway into the future in which customary values could be combined with development. Father Walter Lini advocated a small-is-beautiful approach to development. When he lived in Longana, he sought to put these ideas into practice through the establishment of the Longana Peoples' Center which would teach new skills such as sandal-making using simple technology.

Against this background, it is not surprising that Longanans are keen consumers of development who also maintain a deep commitment to customary ways. They kill tusked pigs and take rank as their ancestors did; they exchange woven mats by the hundreds at traditional weddings; but they hold Holy Communion before the pig killings and are married in the church as well as in custom. They listen to the radio, ask questions of visiting government workers, gripe about taxes, and are always eager to weigh the pros and cons of a new development program. Basically, Longanans have confidence in their government and turn to it as a source of opportunities for those local people who want to try new forms of productive activity.

Port Olry and Nagriamel

Such is not the case in Port Olry, where dealings with the government are viewed with deep suspicion and, wherever possible, avoided. This opposition to government in general, and to the government in power in particular, can be traced directly to the 1980 rebellion in which Port Olry was the last stronghold to surrender. But a trenchant resistance to Europeans has been characteristic of Santo islanders from the beginning, and the people of Port Olry include descendants of the residents of Big Bay who greeted the explorer Quiros with suspicion and hostility.

The supremacy of customary land claims over the rights of expatriate land developers was an issue about which the ni-Vanuatu on the east coast of Santo felt particularly strongly. The 65 km from Luganville to Port Olry is a chain of old plantations, with links formed of fences whose posts have taken root and grown into trees. The people of Port Olry, only 12 km from Peacock's proposed American colony in Hog Harbor, were among the first to lend their support to the Nagriamel movement. They were also among the first to leave Nagriamel when the land issue seemed compromised.

Jimmy Stevens, a plump, graybearded man in his sixties who is said to be descended from a Tongan princess and a Scottish seaman,[16] now serves a life sentence in the Port Vila prison for leading the secessionist rebellion that took place, mainly in Santo, on the eve of independence in 1980. Stevens had worked for the Americans during the war and amassed considerable prestige among islanders through redistributing among them, Robin Hood-style, the hospital supplies to which he had access through his job. Later he worked for a Santo trader, and then drove a bulldozer for the British administration. An accident with the bulldozer permanently injured his right leg and embittered Stevens because the British failed to provide any compensation.

In 1963, Stevens formed Nagriamel, which took its name from two leaves, "na garia" and "na mele," that are closely associated with customary ceremonial activity and so with peacetime. (Participants contributing pigs to a graded society ceremony had to be confident that they would not be attacked on the path or at the event.) Stevens' movement, focussed on the issue of land, attracted a following unprecedented in Vanuatu, bringing together pagans and Christians who had been fragmented by sectarian differences under the aegis of a traditional heritage. Over time, Nagriamel came to stand for free enterprise and individualism as well as customary landrights. This was consistent with the Santo peoples' orientation, but it would be naive to see this emphasis as one that ni-Vanuatu brought to Nagriamel. The emphasis on free enterprise and individualism became part of Nagriamel largely because of the influence of American businessmen who saw in Stevens an opportunity to create their own kingdom.[17]

Nagriamel is a movement filled with contradictions. While the ni-Vanuatu right to the dark bush was the charter for Nagriamel, Stevens turned to the two sectors that had most usurped ni-Vanuatu land as his movement weakened under competition from the Vanuaaku Pati in the early 1970s.

First, Stevens allowed Nagriamel to be courted by the French administration. The French returned some of the alienated land that had catalyzed Nagriamel's formation. French settlers of mixed blood began to see Nagriamel as less of a threat to their interests than the Vanuaaku Pati; they concurred with the French administration in feeling that success for Nagriamel would buy time for the gradual resolution of land disputes and establishment of a strong elite of francophone ni-Vanuatu who could preserve French education and culture in the islands. Thus Nagriamel and the Vanuaaku Pati came to recreate the Condominium's division between France and Britain.

For the Port Olry people, Nagriamel's alliance with French interests was a perfectly acceptable addition to the movement's emphasis on customary landrights. Port Olry is a francophone, Catholic community whose residents felt that French education would be endangered by an independent Vanuatu under the leadership of the Anglophone Vanuaaku Pati.

The direction in which Stevens turned in his second attempt to bolster support for Nagriamel, however, was highly unpopular in Port Olry. In fact, it drove the villagers from the Nagriamel camp. The target of Nagriamel's demands for the return of customary land had always been the dark bush; by 1974 Stevens argued that it had never been his intention to demand the return of cultivated land, only the uncleared dark bush. On this basis, he was able to justify an alliance with Eugene Peacock, the developer whose activities near Hog Harbor and elsewhere had caused such furor among ni-Vanuatu. Stevens signed a letter to a Hawaiian senator affirming Peacock's right to develop the land, receiving in return—somewhat ironically in view of Stevens' earlier accident—the gift of a reconditioned bulldozer from Peacock.

People in the Port Olry area, disenchanted by Stevens' pact with Peacock, joined a splinter movement called Tabwemassana, named for the highest mountain on Santo. Eventually, Tabwemassana was part of a coalition of movements supporting Stevens and Nagriamel in the rebellion. Armed with shotguns and bows and arrows, Port Olry residents were among those who tore up and down Luganville's wide street terrifying the citizenry at the outset of the revolt. And they were the last to surrender. The Papua New Guinea Defence Force, whose aid Fr. Walter Lini enlisted to quell the insurgency, finally pacified the area, firing shells at the village and strafing the shore with machine gun fire in response to the wounding of two of the military men by sniper fire.

Although the Port Olry people raised a white flag, they surrendered as little of their independence as possible. They have remained skeptical of the government, wary of outsiders—white or ni-Vanuatu— and stubbornly individualistic. Like many Santo people, they feel that neither the Condominium nor the Republic of Vanuatu has adequately represented their interests or developed their island. Whatever development is to occur, the Port Olry residents feel, must be accomplished by individuals who seek a profit, who succeed on their own initiative or fail through their own shortcomings.

Longana and Port Olry Compared

The differences between Port Olry and Longana in terms of their political history should be quite apparent by now. Anglophone, Anglican Longana was staunchly behind the Vanuaaku Pati and, following that party's rise to power, tends to trust the government. Francophone, Catholic Port Olry backed Nagriamel, became disillusioned with Stevens' handling of the land question, but joined with his movement in fierce support of the Santo Rebellion. Once the rebellion was quashed and the Vanuaaku Pati came to rule Vanuatu, Port Olry people have stayed as clear of dealings with the government as possible.

While these differences are profound and will shape the future of both places as they have shaped the historical past, the contrasts between Port Olry and Longana should not be allowed to obscure their similarities. Both Longana and Port Olry are matrilineal societies with a tradition of killing and exchanging tusked pigs: in Longana, such customs are still practiced; in Port Olry at least they are still remembered. Both places were deeply influenced by missions located within or near their borders; both have disputed their mission's right to local land, and residents in both situations have appreciated the contribution of mission schools and healthcare to improving the quality of their lives. In both situations, political sentiments have been honed by contrast—and conflict—with neighbors of a different political persuasion. The antagonism between Catholic, Francophone Port Olry and Anglican, Anglophone Hog Harbour is well-known in Santo, and erupted in fighting during the rebellion. In Longana, about one third of the population supported Nagriamel. These supporters were not dispersed among the population at large; rather, they were members of settlements that had joined the Church of Christ at about the same time as other Longanans were baptized as Anglicans in the early 20th century. Conflict between the Vanuaaku Pati supporters and Nagriamel was expressed in blockaded roads and heated arguments, but never became as violent as the Port Olry–Hog Harbour contretemps.

Both Port Olry and Longana have earned reputations as places that are more oriented toward business than some other rural areas. Stores, trucks, cattle, and cocoa supplement income from copra in both areas. Port Olry also provides vegetables for the town market, and because of its good road links to Luganville the village's involvement in commerce is greater than Longana's. But in both areas there are some who successfully seek to earn a lot of money by local standards—perhaps $10,000 a year, with no income taxes or mortgage to pay and home-grown food to eat. Such individuals buy video cassette players and designer sunglasses; they can pay cash for an outboard motor and a boat.

Obviously, not everyone earns such an income; what may be less obvious is that not everyone wants to. Port Olry and Longana have more people than in most parts of Vanuatu who are keen businesspeople with an interest in development and a talent for making money. But many individuals in both places so far have maintained their involvement with capitalist markets on a less regular basis and a smaller scale. As I have discussed elsewhere,[18] such people, who constitute the majority of rural ni-Vanuatu, prefer to perform non-market activities; they only make copra when they need money, and their perceived need for money is not great, being confined to payment of school fees, purchases of basic goods (such as clothes, kerosene, rice, etc.), and an occasional trip to another island.

Self-reliance is a concept that is relevant to both Port Olry and Longana, and to the businesspeople and intermittent producers in both communities. One reason for the concept's broad applicability is that it contains multiple, and contradictory meanings. Consider Vanuatu's commitment to achieve self-reliance by 1990. This could be accomplished by increasing exports to the point where they can be expected to pay for the country's imports for the foreseeable future. Alternatively, self-reliance could be achieved by ensuring that villagers can look after enough of their own needs to reduce the volume of imports into the country. Both approaches to self-reliance can generate increases in income-producing activity; but in the first instance that activity must focus on exportable commodities such as copra whereas in the second instance the emphasis must be on production for local consumption, such as taro. Yet efforts to achieve these two forms of self-reliance need not come into conflict. As we shall see in the next chapter, the Village Fisheries Development Program has the potential to work toward both dimensions of self-sufficiency and to work with both kinds of producers—the businessperson and the intermittent money-earner—while smoothing over the contradictions that are built into the concept of self-reliance.

Notes

1. MacClancy (1981:36).

2. I have borrowed the phrase, "they came for sandalwood" from Dorothy Shineberg's (1967) historical account by the same name.

3. Ibid.

4. MacClancy 1981:45–46

5. Ibid.45.

6. See for example Corris (1970) and Scarr (1967a, 1967b). I have also prepared an unpublished manuscript on ni-Vanuatu and the labor trade (Rodman 1977).

7. See Michael Gilding (1982) and M. Rodman (1987c, Chapter 2) for further information about this attack.

8. Bislama is a creolized local version of the Melanesian pidgin that developed during the labor trade. It is the most widely shared language in Vanuatu, a country with greater linguistic diversity than any other country in the world (105–110 languages among a population of about 128,000)(Connell 1983:1).

9. MacClancy (1981:88). See also M. Rodman (1987c, Chapter 5) for a

description of current practices of employing local labor among Ambae smallholder plantation owners, and analysis of the implications of this practice for social differentiation.

10. See W. Rodman (1979, 1985) for analyses of the islanders' creative responses to the Condominium and to independence in matters of law.

11. MacClancy (1981:110).

12. Lane (1971:257).

13. By 1984, Vanuatu was self-sufficient in beef and exports of beef accounted for 10.8 percent of exports by value (Vanuatu 1984a:98–99).

14. Beasant (1984:45).

15. Cited in Beasant's account of the events leading up to the Santo rebellion of 1980 (1984:45).

16. Ibid. 1984:18.

17. The story of American involvement in the Santo Rebellion is intriguingly recounted in *The Coconut War* (Shears 1980). John Beasant, who was Fr. Walter Lini's Press Secretary during the uprising, gives a more serious analysis of the American co-optation of Jimmy Stevens, calling the Santo story "a paradigm case of the worst aspects of imperialism" (1984:152).

18. M. Rodman (1984, 1986).

5

FISHERIES DEVELOPMENT

Appropriately, the Fisheries Department of the Vanuatu government has a fine view of the water. Set on a flat strip of land reclaimed from the sea, the long, single-storey white building houses administrative offices, research facilities, a workshop, and a classroom. Through the office windows, one can keep an eye on the department's small fishing boats moored at the buoys just off shore.

From this vantage point, most of Port Vila lies along the harbor to the right. A commercial and plantation settlement since the 1880s, Port Vila grew into a small town (1986 pop. 14,184) once it became the administrative center of the Condominium in the early 20th century. The shoreline stretching for about 1 km from the Fisheries Department to the center of town is dotted with wharves and businesses, waterfront restaurants and an open-air market. In places, the lush green of a jungle kept at bay bursts through; a low hanging branch from a banyan tree extends out over the hulk of an abandoned yacht at the harbor's edge; flame trees in Christmas colors rise above government offices whose shuttered verandas evoke the colonial past. Some of this past is still architecturally in evidence, but much has disappeared. The Rossi Hotel on the far edge of town from the Fisheries Department continues to earn its reputation as one of the last of the old South Pacific watering holes and the best place in town to watch the sunset.

The focal point of the harbor view from the bar at the Rossi is Iririki Island which used to be the site of the British Resident Commissioner's home. When we first arrived in Port Vila in 1969, coming ashore in a lighter from the French steamer *Caledonien* because there was no wharf in those days, Iririki was also the site of the British hospital; canoes and dinghies ferried the patients across a few hundred meters of iridescent water from a wharf near the Burns Philp store on the town shore. Now Iririki overflows with "native" bungalows, providing accommodation for hundreds of tourists as part of an international resort that opened in 1986.

On the other side of the Fisheries Department, a narrow coastal shelf is overshadowed by cliffs. A few expatriate residents of Vila live in houses that peek through the jungle atop the cliffs, enjoying views of the harbor and town that would make anyone want to spend their lives in Vanuatu. Below them lies the big wharf where a cruise ship docks every week or two, its white hull and hoards of tourists welcome but out of scale with the rest of the scene. Between the cruise ship and the Fisheries complex, the government wharf accommodates inter-island ships with names such as the *Euphrosyne* that have been used for government vessels since the old days of the Condominium. The sleek, dark patrol vessel *Mala* (The Hawk), which is the only ship that serves a naval function for the Vanuatu Mobile Force, is moored at this wharf, waiting for such excitement as the day in 1982 when it apprehended Jimmy Stevens as he made his escape from prison in a glass-bottomed boat.[1]

Port Vila seems quiet only in comparison to a western urban lifestyle. Rural islanders who come to the capital find a rapid pace of life unknown elsewhere in the archipelago; overseas volunteers anticipating a quiet backwater in need of their skills find a cosmopolitan town with croissants, Perrier, and four distinct ten-minute rush hours. The working day starts early (at 7:30 am) and ends early (at 4:30 pm); everything closes for lunch from 11:30 am until 1:30 or 2:00 pm. In spite of, or perhaps because of, the short business day the atmosphere in government offices can be frenetic as office personnel try to process the building of a country.

For the Fisheries Department, this building process seemed to start from scratch.[*] The department was created jointly by the government and the United Nations Development Program in December 1978 as part of the process of setting up administrative structures in anticipation of independence. As the Fisheries Department moved into operation, the level of fishing activity in the islands seemed limited and, when compared to other Pacific islands countries, relatively undeveloped. The department sought to change this situation, making the fisheries sector productive as soon as possible.[2] The objectives of

---

[*] For readers new to the subject, "fishery" is the term used to describe a complex system involving, first, fishermen using similar techniques; second, a resource consisting of particular kinds of fish in the same ecological niche; and, third, a market (Epple 1977:174).

the department concerning coastal fisheries were to (1) "provide the necessary infrastructure, training and facilities to make fishing a viable and attractive occupation; (2) develop the capacity to produce sufficient fresh fish to satisfy local demand; (3) develop, where feasible, small-scale export-oriented fisheries."[3] The department also had a mandate to conduct research on fisheries resources, and, in the long run, to develop an industrial fishery based in Vanuatu to catch, and possibly process, tuna.[4]

Initially, all of these tasks fell to the Director of Fisheries and nine staff, only three of whom had extensive professional experience. By the time I began conducting my research for this book in August 1985, the Director told me that the staff now included 32 people representing 7 nationalities: Australia, Britain, Canada, France, the Netherlands, New Zealand, and Vanuatu. Philippine experts helped construct fish aggregating devices. Japanese, through the Overseas Fisheries Cooperation Foundation, assisted with village fisheries development, and Japanese aid made possible the establishment of fish markets in Port Vila and Santo. By 1986, Danish volunteers would join the department's ranks. Funding and technical assistance for coastal fisheries development have come mainly from the European Economic Community, the United Kingdom, Canada, Australia, New Zealand and the International Human Assistance Program.[5]

I used to walk to the Fisheries Department. From the main road, a street mined with potholes leads down the hill to the harbor shore, a distance of perhaps half a km. I enjoyed the walk, the humid air pungent with frangipani and just a hint of exhaust fumes during what we came to call "rush minute." A row of workers' housing lines the street. The yards seemed always to be neatly swept bare and filled with little girls playing cards under the trees.[6] Women lay on mats in the shade, tending babies or resting. The atmosphere was what one might expect of a sidestreet in a tropical island town.

When I opened the door to the Fisheries Department at the bottom of the street, I entered another world. One measure of the department's success was that the building was bursting at the seams. When I began my work, the director of the Village Fisheries Development Program (VFDP) shared an office with the program's field officer, a fisheries officer, and a shortwave radio which many people came in to use for communication with fisheries personnel in the outer islands and, when the telephone was inoperative as seemed often to be the case, with the Fisheries Department office in Luganville. In some offices, there really was not enough room to open the door. Where the door could be opened, it seemed to open continually as one person after another came and went, trying to get something done as soon as possible. The building had been designed with more attention to cross-ventilation than to the needs of bureaucracy, so that a surge of wind accompanied every opening door and sent a cloud of papers into the air. Scattered photographs of new orange skiffs, a proud volunteer posing next to a 6-foot marlin, and a master fisherman setting off a safety flare (that allegedly landed in the British Petroleum depot behind the department), would settle to the floor along with project documents, job descriptions, salary information, requests for icemakers, and bits of fishing line. Like everyone working in the department, I soon became conditioned to slap both hands on my papers at the first sound of the door unlatching; perhaps it was symbolic that there was always more paper to blow away than there were hands to hold it down.

Village Fisheries Project Applications

For all this, the Village Fisheries Development Program is not especially bureaucratic. The paperwork involved in starting a project is relatively simple, consisting of not much more than a one-page application for a loan from the Development Bank. The procedure that has been established for dealing with project requests tries to encourage the serious applicant while discouraging others. Typically, an islander contacts the department—in person, or more often through a letter or through a relative who works in town—to inquire about starting a fishing project involving a single, small boat with an outboard motor and fishing gear. Ice is seldom a consideration since such projects aim at sales directly from the beach to the consumer. Such a project cost about $6,500 to establish in 1985.

Applicants are encouraged in several ways. First, as much as 40 percent of the project costs can be covered by a Development Bank loan with a three-year term and a 4 percent commission fee. Moreover, applicants are eligible for a grant using funds from aid donors to cover as much as 50 percent of the cost of setting up the project. Finally, they are made aware that outboard motor fuel is available to fishermen through the department at about half the retail price; this is possible because of duty-free status obtained to encourage village fishermen. These three kinds of assistance were built into the VFDP to provide an impetus for rapid development. Without such support, it was felt, "the development of a viable fishery might take many years or never become established at all."[7]

But applicants are also discouraged, in an effort to weed out those who would not succeed if their projects were funded. First, the department stresses that the applicant must come up with at least 10 percent of the cost of the project as a "personal contribution." In the early days of the VFDP, personal contributions usually amounted to $1,000 because the type of boat then in use was more expensive, but even now $650 is enough to give some applicants pause. There has been a tendency to increase the amount that an applicant is encouraged to contribute in order both to reduce the initial loan and to intensify the fisherman's commitment to the success of the project. Second, applicants are told that they would be expected to participate in a 4-week fisherman's training course in Port Vila. Third, they are instructed that they must file records of their fishing activity with the department on a regular basis in order to receive duty-free fuel. Often, an applicant is discouraged after the first encounter with a representative of the VFDP.

One custom that has emerged in the VFDP is to take seriously any applicant who comes back a second time. Another is to expect older, married men to be more successful with new projects than young men. But Fisheries Department personnel recognize that they cannot always predict which projects are most likely to succeed. For example, the department was reluctant to assist a group of young, unmarried Tongoan men to set up a fishing project. The VFDP manager had great misgivings about the project's chances of success, but he had a damaged Alia catamaran on his hands for which he had no other use. So he said the Tongoans could have the catamaran if they raised a couple of thousand dollars as their personal contribution. To the manager's surprise the Tongoan boys have done very well indeed.

The department's criteria of success and self-reliance are evident in the manager's assessment of this Tongoan project's surprising performance. The first thing that a project must do to establish its viability is to repay the Development Bank loan within three years. Subsequently, in the eyes of the manager of the VFDP, persistence is the key criterion of success; if a boat is in working order and used for fishing, even somewhat irregularly, that project can be labelled a success. The young Tongoans kept their boat going despite the fact that it was not in good shape when they acquired it. They worked hard. And they proved to be loyal to the department. For all these reasons, they could be considered a success.

It seemed to me that a project's loyalty is crucial to the way it is viewed by the department. As an example of the Tongoan project's successfulness, I was told that they sell all their fish to the Port Vila fish market (which is closely linked to the fisheries department) and that they have gone to new grounds where the department asked them to fish. To some extent, the department can compel loyalty using duty-free fuel as a powerful incentive for fishermen to go fishing, to file records of their fishing activity, and to sell their catch to the fish markets in Vila and Santo. But the department does not take such loyalty for granted and values it highly. Conversely, for a project to be deemed disloyal is a serious criticism that may be accompanied by a withdrawal of departmental support. The high value that the department places on what it views as loyalty can be a source of conflict with local people for whom the concept sometimes seems opaque or inappropriate in the context of fisheries development.

The example of the young Tongoans also illustrates that elements of the model I presented earlier in the context of a Melanesian paradigm of success are shared by expatriates in the Fisheries Department. Like the traditional metaphor of a fish trap that contains a successful man's unexpected wealth, the Tongoan project's success was all the greater because no one outside the project expected it to perform well.

CUSO Volunteers

Although many small projects have succeeded on their own, others have had volunteers to assist them. Many of these volunteers have been Canadians, because CUSO has been involved in village fisheries development in Vanuatu since the planning stage in 1981. Until December 1980, when CUSO became simply CUSO, it had been an acronym that stood for Canadian University Service Overseas. CUSO is a non-government organization which serves as Canada's volunteer agency in overseas development. Each year CUSO places about 200 people in less-developed countries where they serve at least two years in various positions. CUSO places about 10 "cooperants," as the volunteers are called, in Vanuatu each year. The CUSO-Vanuatu program is coordinated by a Field Staff Office in Port Vila.

So far, CUSO has tried to recruit about 3 volunteers each year in fisheries. The first fisheries cooperant arrived in 1981, and a total of 14 CUSO volunteers had worked with the Fisheries Department by the end of 1985. I had the good fortune to meet 10 of them over the years and to talk with 8 of them for this project, as well as with the Field Staff Officers and non-fisheries CUSO cooperants.

While 4 of the cooperants have served as Fisheries Officers or Master Fishermen based in Port Vila or Santo, most of the volunteers have spent at least part of their time as Village Fisheries Advisors. CUSO has considered the position of Village Fisheries Advisor to be one of the most difficult postings in the country because of the variety of social and technical skills required. Advisors have been expected to teach new fishing techniques, to run short courses on the use, maintenance and repair of fishing gear and outboard motors, to investigate new projects and assist established ones with such matters as bookkeeping, fish storage and marketing. Although a Village Fisheries Advisor (VFA) should have at least five years of commercial fishing experience, preferably as an owner and operator of a fishing boat, CUSO staff have found that "life experience" is as important as fishing expertise in making a successful advisor. Experience travelling and working overseas has helped the most effective cooperants to develop a relaxed attitude toward living in a village. VFAs who respond to advertisements like the one in Figure 3 must be independent, self-motivated, and very patient.

They must learn to understand that local attitudes toward work are different from their own; they cannot expect to arrive on an island and find all the villagers lined up on the beach ready to go fishing. They must be able to cope with seemingly capricious shortages of supplies; one week the country is out of shackles, two weeks later there are shackles by the dozen but no small bolts. They must be willing and able to work themselves out of a job, so that the local fishermen are self-reliant by the time the volunteer leaves.

The Fisheries Department and the volunteers agree about the basic criteria for a successful fishing project. Repayment of the loan and persistence, even at a low level of activity, are key indicators of a project's success. Yet the relationship between the volunteers and the department is not always tranquil, and often the differences between them represent conflicting assumptions about *what kind* of development is desirable, and about *how* fisheries development should be achieved.

Fundamentally, these are questions of self-reliance. Does the acquisition of a freezer encourage self-reliance because, in and of itself, it is a "free" piece of equipment provided by a foreign donor that otherwise might have to be purchased with hard currency? Or is it unnecessary cargo that will be of little or no use in the islands and will simply consume expensive fuel, then breakdown never to be repaired because of a lack of spare parts? Too often the latter is the case. Does a bigger boat increase self-reliance by allowing fishermen to increase their catches? Yes, in the few cases of island fishermen who are fully committed to fishing regularly for the market. But far more often a bigger boat would actually hinder an islander from achieving a self-reliant position; it would mean that he had to go fishing fulltime, cutting off other options such as gardening that might support him if the fishing was bad. Generally, the fisheries department's approach to development tends to regard "cargo" as beneficial; the CUSO volunteers prefer to emphasize a simpler technology; and islanders, while enjoying the cargo, are wary of finding themselves in a position where they would have to do nothing but catch fish.

HOW WOULD YOU LIKE TO TRY A NEW TACK...

FISHING
IN THE
SOUTH PACIFIC

CUSO requires experienced fishermen to fill several positions in Vanuatu for a minimum of two years. Salaries are very low but adequate ($5000 to $7000 Canadian/year), and the living conditions are basic but the experience will last a lifetime ...

FIGURE 3
Recruiting Brochure for CUSO-Vanuatu Fisheries Cooperants

The differences between the department and the volunteers have intensified as the volunteers have become less central to the planning process. In the early days of the Fisheries Department, CUSO cooperants played crucial roles in shaping the village fisheries development program. One volunteer told me that in 1982 everyone knew what everyone else was doing, so you could talk about whether to get an icemaker or a truck and help to decide if these things were needed before they were bought. Increasingly, the cooperants have detected a "more is better" orientation in the department that they dislike. In turn, the department has at times found the volunteers to be too independent, too full of "grand designs" for development in the islands.

The complex and dynamic relationship between those in charge of fisheries development and the CUSO volunteers will be explored in later chapters. Here, I will introduce only one issue which has been the focus for a certain amount of conflict, as well as a lot of hard work, involving the department, the villagers and the volunteers, namely the development of a fish marketing infrastructure.

Fish Markets

Plans to establish a fish market in Port Vila were made in 1981, at the same time as the first efforts were being made to develop village fisheries. Some of the same personnel were involved in both operations, and the market was seen as a way of providing support for the village program in several ways. The market would provide a buyer for catches that were bigger than the villagers' needs; it would offer stable prices to fishermen; and it would serve as a showcase "shop window" for fisheries development programs in Vanuatu.[8]

Initially, plans called for a second facility in Luganville that would simply provide cold storage for fish on their way to Port Vila; but a CUSO volunteer and regular Fisheries personnel recognized the need for a fully operating fish market in Santo. The plan was revised and the markets were constructed in 1982–83, financed by Japanese aid. The Port Vila market, called *Natai* which means "seafood" in the local Ifira language, opened in May 1983 on a site near the fresh produce market. Two months later, the Santo enterprise, known as "Santofish," began trading operations in a small, screened building on the bank of the Sarakata River next to the town market.

Port Vila Fisheries, a company wholly owned by the Vanuatu government, runs both markets. The company promised to buy any fish of good quality. The price paid to fishermen was set on the basis of a survey of the retail and wholesale prices for fresh fish prevailing in other stores, with a view towards yielding a return to the fishermen that would be adequate to ensure that they continued to produce for the new fish markets. Fishermen who obtained their fuel through the Fisheries Department were expected to sell their product to Port Vila Fisheries regardless of whether they might obtain a higher price by selling directly to hotels or to Chinese buyers. Private buyers' prices fluctuate and there is no guarantee to buy all the fish supplied, so a fisherman's loyalty to the department assured him of a stable market for his fish.

While there have been times when the fish markets were poorly supplied, and calls went out to the projects in the islands for more fish, the most common problem has been one of oversupply. In January 1984 and again in early 1986, exceptionally good fishing conditions led to bonanza catches. In Santo, the excess fish from the 1984 catch were frozen and stored at the South Pacific Fishing Company plant for later sale. But when I last visited Port Vila in February 1986, no solution had been found for the problem of what to do with the recent surplus of fish, some of which had suffered damage in the freezing process.[9]

The question of how much potential demand there is for fish in Vanuatu has yet to receive a clear answer. The difficulty and expense of transporting fish in the islands pose ongoing obstacles to meeting, and encouraging, demand. Air Melanesiae became a viable means of transporting fish caught in the outer islands to market once the problem of packaging the fish adequately was resolved. (Smelly fish, leaky bags, hot days, and small passenger aircraft were a combination that made initial relations between the department and the airline unpleasant at times!)[10] But the high price of airfreight in the islands has meant that only premium species are worth sending to market. In some instances, villagers have felt that they are sending the best fish to market and feeding themselves on less desirable species. But in other cases, villagers say that they do not regard the premium snappers and poulet as the best eating fish anyway.

There is a danger that an effort to achieve self-reliance for the country as a whole will draw fish away from the island consumers and so affect local self-reliance. Another threat to local self-reliance comes from the fact that commercial fishing may lead islanders away from other activities, such as gardening, through which they have maintained a degree of independence from the marketplace. Further, commercial fishing requires inputs to production that are expensive— outboard motors, fuel—and that therefore require the fishermen not just to catch fish but also to sell their catch in order to cover their costs.

The market, then, provides ni-Vanuatu fishermen with security, but it exacts a price. Working with villagers in the outer islands, CUSO volunteers are particularly aware of the contradiction between local and national self-reliance. They can see that self-reliance at the village level involves maintenance of choices: whether to go fishing or do something else; whether to fish from a canoe or a motorboat; whether to consume, give away, and/or sell one's catch. So a project can be a success in terms of increasing local self-reliance if it gives villagers new options. A CUSO volunteer would be reluctant to say that a project wasn't successful just because the islanders only went out fishing occasionally. The point is rather that because of the project the people now have a choice—to fish or not—and now have the wherewithal to catch as much as 100 kg of fresh fish if they want to hold a feast.

While non-CUSO personnel in the Fisheries Department would agree with this view, they also seek to build the foundations for another kind of self-reliance, one that potentially conflicts with the local kind. They need to encourage rural islanders to participate in the new markets for fresh fish in order to establish a steady supply of fish to urban consumers and to develop an export trade in fish that will offset some of the country's imports. The process of developing the fish marketing infrastructure is difficult and slow, but eventually some of those who fish commercially will be led away from a simple commodity form of production, in which the fisherman in many ways is really his own boss, into a capitalist mode of production in which the fisherman must work regularly and sell his fish to cover the costs of operating a commercial fishing boat.

From the perspective of the full-freezers of Port Vila Fisheries, the business already is pressing against the ceiling of the domestic market. Consumer resistance seems likely if retail prices are raised above current levels. In September 1985, poulet and snapper retail prices in Port Vila were $2.90 per kg for whole gilled and gutted fish, $4.80 for steaks, and $6.80 for filets. Although mixed whole fish sold for $1.80 per kilo, there were complaints that the fish market was priced beyond the means of most ni-Vanuatu residents in the capital. Santofish retail prices were lower ($2.00, $2.40, and $5.00 for whole, steaked, and fileted premium fish, respectively), partly because their price to the fishermen was set 50 cents lower per kg than in Port Vila.

Lowering prices in the markets to encourage demand has seemed to be out of the question. The difference of 90 cents in Port Vila and 50 cents in Santo between the price paid to fishermen and the retail price per kg for snapper and poulet has not been enough for the fish markets to earn a profit given the volume of sales. Through 1985, Port Vila Fisheries sales were about $300,000 per year; the manager estimated that an annual volume of about $500,000 would be necessary for the company to make a profit given existing costs. Electricity alone cost an estimated 41 cents for each kg of fish handled. Other costs included "market risk" (bad debts), insurance, salaries, repairs and maintenance, packaging, promotion, depreciation, and storage. The spoilage rate was less than 1 percent.

Export Potential

An interest in increasing the volume of business without altering prices to either the producers or urban consumers, has led Port Vila Fisheries to explore the development of export markets for Vanuatu fish. While the hope is to increase the volume of fish handled by Port Vila Fisheries, this increase would be small by world standards; the strategy is different from that followed elsewhere in the insular Pacific. For example, Solomon Islands established a tuna fishing industry on a 50/50 basis with the Japanese in order to benefit from high volume resources of fish in the open ocean of Solomon Islands' 200 mile zone. Because the market prospects for such an enterprise no longer seem promising, and the benefits to the Solomon Islanders seem questionable, Vanuatu chose to follow an alternate course, emphasizing an exclusive, top quality product for restaurant consumption.

Vanuatu's niche is defined by the excellence of its fish. In order to recover the high costs of catching, storing and transporting fish in Vanuatu, the incipient export trade seeks to attain a high standard in presenting and packaging the "creme de la creme" of deepwater snappers, species that are attractive to international, first class restaurants.

The technique known as *iki jimi* has helped Vanuatu fishermen achieve the goal of a high quality, attractive product. Introduced into Vanuatu by the manager of Port Vila Fisheries, the technique is a variant of ones used centuries earlier by some Pacific islanders and by Portuguese fishermen who walloped cod on the head as they caught the fish.[11] This way of killing the fish kept it fresh longer than other methods then available. With a mixture of ice and saltwater, called a slurry, in which to plunge the fish as soon as it is killed, the technique can be made even more effective.

Who would want to eat a steer that died a natural death? Like cattle, fish that are killed with a quick blow to the head yield better quality flesh and deteriorate more slowly than fish that are allowed to die slowly. At fish markets in Japan, the manager of Port Vila Fisheries observed that fishmongers would kill live fish as they were sold, slitting their throats and tails. He reasoned that stabbing a fish in the brain would achieve the same result. *Iki jimi* is a Japanese term invented to describe the technique that is used currently in the Pacific in which the fish is killed as soon as it is caught by stabbing it in the brain. The combination of this killing technique with rapid immersion in a saltwater and ice slurry seals the fish and preserves it without chemicals by immediately closing off the capillaries. No waste matter escapes into the circulatory or nervous systems; no intestinal juices seep into the flesh of the fish. Killing a fish by the *iki jimi* technique extends its shelf life to as much as 28 days. With proper chilling, the fish remains in perfect condition. But, as in a fairy tale, there is one admonition that must be followed or the spell will be broken: one must never touch a fish killed with the *iki jimi* technique after it is chilled, for the fingerprint will remain as an indentation that does not disappear.

Vanuatu's first trial exports of frozen fish were sent to Australia and New Caledonia in 1983/84. Samples of chilled fish have been sent to Australia, Japan, and England. On the first anniversary of the opening of the fish markets that had been funded with Japanese aid, Port Vila Fisheries was able to send a gift of Vanuatu's finest fish with Prime Minister Lini who was attending a conference in Japan at that time. The fish chosen for the gift was *Etelis coruscans*, a red snapper with a long, plume-like tail (see Figure 4).

An effort was made to catch snappers that were no longer than 520 cm so that they would fit in special fish boxes for export. These fish would have commanded prices of about $16 per kg in Japan at that time, and their net weight is about 20 percent greater than fish that have been gilled and gutted.

In order to support an export trade in top quality snappers, Vanuatu will require a second stage, or a "second generation" of fishermen with larger boats 10–12 m long, inboard diesel engines, and refrigeration.

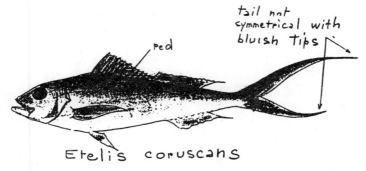

FIGURE 4
Drawing of *Etelis Coruscans* (Red Snapper)

Four such boats would be adequate to supply about 500 kg per week of snapper killed with the *iki jimi* technique and airfreighted to Japan. This volume would be enough to make the trade profitable to Vanuatu if the Japanese buyers paid at least $9.00 per kg.[12]

Although plans for an export industry must look toward a second generation, Vanuatu's first generation of commercial fishermen is still in the process of emerging and these are the islanders on whom the day to day activities of the Village Fisheries Development Program focus. By the time I left Vanuatu in December 1985, the number of village fisheries projects in various stages of operation had reached nearly 100. Each project is unique, ranging in size from a single motorized canoe to the Port Olry association with its 15 motorboats. Early projects were organized somewhat differently from later ones; an initial preference for Alia catamarans was rejected in favor of single-hulled Hartleys. Yet the overall similarities between the projects are considerable, reflecting the fact that they all seek to catch the same kinds of fish employing the same techniques as those used in the first projects in the program.

Fisheries Research

The Fisheries Department first began to receive requests from communities and individuals wanting to start their own fishing projects in February 1981, when the people of Paama Island requested assistance in establishing a project. Paama had been among the islands visited by a team from the South Pacific Commission that introduced villagers to techniques for catching deep water snapper on handlines and began an assessment of the potential for this type of fishing in Vanuatu. Early results were encouraging. On one trip the average catch rate was 8.2 kg of fish per reel hour, among the highest obtained in the region.[13] Later research conducted by the French research organization ORSTOM averaged 3 kg per reel hour at depths between 80 and 320 meters.

The Etelidae are the most common species caught on the deep reef slopes in the tropical Pacific, comprising 62 percent of the fish caught in the ORSTOM study.[14] These are the snappers and "poulet fish," of which *Etelis carbunculus, Etelis coruscans, Pristipomoides multidens,* and *Pristipomoides flavipinnis* are the major species. The ORSTOM and SPC research has assessed the depths at which these species are most likely to be caught, finding that at night there is an overall upward movement by 40 to 80 meters of species that live in the daytime at depths between 80 and 240 meters, where most of the fishing effort is concentrated. Some seasonal variation was identified, with maximum catch rates occurring from February to July. The different Etelidae species favor a variety of bottom types. For example, the *Etelis* species favor rocky bottoms at the foot of submarine cliffs while the *Pristipomoides* species are most often found on gentle slopes, except for *Pristipomoides filamentosus* which have been seen in large, active schools on the edge of sheer reef drop-offs.[15]

Overall, research indicates that deep water resources are more sensitive to overfishing than are the fish within the reef for several reasons. First, the diversity of species is less in the deeper water. Second, the deeper water is less rich in nutrients and so supports fewer fish per hectare of surface area than the shallower areas. Third, the larger species that live in the deeper water such as the *Etelis* spp. grow very slowly.

The age of a fish can be estimated in much the same way as the age of a tree. Daily growth rings can be seen on otoliths, which are thin cross-sections prepared from segments of fish bone.[16] Analysis of otoliths reveals that some of the snappers caught on handlines are as much as 20–30 years old. This means that an *Etelis* fish is much older than a *Pristipomoides* of the same size, and some *Etelis* species are caught before they reach sexual maturity using the same hooks and lines that catch mature *Pristipomoides*. Obviously, the danger of overfishing is aggravated when there is considerable likelihood of catching fish that have not yet had a chance to reproduce. The ORSTOM study estimated that the mean sustainable yield for fish at depths of 100-400 meters is about 1 kg per hectare per year. Consequently, the mean sustainable yield for Vanuatu as a whole is less than 750 tonnes annually. According to ORSTOM's calculations, this yield would be enough to support 121 Alia-type fishing boats throughout the country.[17]

Although a few ni-Vanuatu had learned to catch *Etelidae* from Polynesians who had settled on Efate Island, deep water handlining was generally unknown in the archipelago. In most instances, the South Pacific Commission (SPC) teams that conducted fishing trials in the late 1970s introduced islanders to varieties of fish they had never seen before. In some places, islanders were skeptical about the new fish, fish of strange colors with eyes that bulged from the pressure of being pulled quickly from the depths. On Tanna, fishermen on an SPC training course in 1979 simply refused to eat the red snapper in their day's catch. They had never seen this species before, but they were convinced on the basis of their experience within the reef that all red fish were inedible. The Tannese watched as the SPC instructor made a fire on the beach and cooked the red snapper. They watched as he alone ate the fish, and they waited to see how long it would take for him to fall sick. Only when the instructor's health was clearly not affected by the strange, new red fish would the Tannese accept it as food.

Deep Water Fishing in Small Boats

For the islanders, the technique used to catch deep water fish was nearly as novel as the fish themselves. There is evidence that Hawaiians traditionally caught snappers and other deep water species using some techniques that are similar to current ones,[18] but the fishery was new to most ni-Vanuatu. It was certainly new to me, and I was eager to accept when one of the volunteers working for the Fisheries Department suggested that we go fishing.

As a tall, Caucasian woman I am used to feeling conspicuous in Vanuatu, but seldom have I felt more so than standing alone on the edge of Luganville's broad, empty street at 4:30 a.m. waiting for a ride to the Fisheries Department. Spotlit by a single street light, I turned up the hood of my yellow slicker against a predawn downpour and hoped that no threats lurked in the darkness beyond my pool of light. A yellow truck with FISERI in black letters on the door stopped for me; I climbed into the cab with Robin Grady,[19] the cooperant who was to be my captain, and met my fellow crew member—an American biologist in his early twenties who was conducting research on the life cycle of coconut crabs. "Okay kids, let's kill some fish!" shouted the captain full of good humor and energy as he parked the truck between the Fisheries Department offices and the water.[20]

By the time I met Robin in 1985 he had served almost two years as a volunteer in Vanuatu. He was an expert fisherman who had owned his own boat before he left Halifax to come to Vanuatu; at some point, he had also served on the lifeboats that stand ready to rescue vessels in trouble off the English coasts. For all his expertise, Robin was carefree and witty. He liked to appear to live for the moment while hinting at a past he preferred to forget. Like all the fisheries volunteers, Robin was darkly tanned, muscular, and usually scruffy. In his late twenties, he was small and fit, with lank brown hair. He enjoyed teasing me about being an anthropologist; I remember his wry grin as he demonstrated what he billed as the invention of shell tools to cut a mooring line when he couldn't find his fishing knife.

We climbed into a dinghy and rowed through the rain toward a small, orange fishing boat moored in the Canal de Segonde a hundred meters off the Fisheries Department's shore. Robin suggested we'd have more fun if we all stayed home and regrouped at the Hotel Santo for a beer at sundown, but we stowed our gear in the fishing boat, a 5 m Hartley-design launch built at the local boatyard.[21] The boats have been popular with local fishermen, and with the Village Fisheries Advisors who have used them in their work. The Hartleys are an improvement over canoes for those fishermen with some money to invest in a boat because they are more seaworthy than canoes, carry a lot more fish, and yet can be fished easily by two people.[22] Half the boats built at the Santo boatyard have been 5 m Hartleys; these boats have proved to be safe—they are virtually unsinkable and so provide some protection against sharks even when the boat is swamped with water—and effective for both trolling and bottom fishing. Their main limitation has been lack of adequate fish-handling space, a problem that is common to small boats.[23] Much of the cockpit is filled with an insulated box containing ice in which the catch is placed.

By 5 a.m. we were underway. Robin stood in the stern, steering the boat and complaining in a good natured way that fishing was a lousy way to earn a living. The last moments before dawn were still and dark, but we could see in shades of gray a monochrome version of a scene that by daylight was all blues and greens. The south arm of the Canal de Segonde stretched before us, the coconut plantations of Aore island to our left and those of South Santo to the right. The broad sweep of water between the two shores was calm that morning. We could have been motoring up a river toward the jungle instead of out to sea. We ate chocolate and watched the sun rise in an ominous sky. Robin pointed to the thunderheads to the east and great V-shaped rays in the western sky; these were signs that a north Atlantic fishermen would have taken seriously. But in Vanuatu, Robin had found, most of the weather signs just don't apply. The day would be fine, Robin promised. I thought he was probably joking.

Just as I was thinking what a dry little boat the Hartley was, we left the shelter of the Canal and entered the choppy waters between Santo and Malekula. For half an hour the launch struggled through waves that appeared to come from all directions. Chocolate for breakfast didn't seem like such a good idea anymore, but Robin still stood in the stern, rain and spray running off his slicker, scanning the sea. Suddenly, he swung the boat sharply around. I thought, with relief I must admit, that we were heading for home because the seas were too rough, but I was wrong. Robin had sighted the fish aggregating device (FAD) off tiny Araki Island at the south entrance to the Canal de Segonde.

The FAD itself looks like a simple raft, but it is an expensive and effective device for attracting fish. The FADs in use in Vanuatu cost about $5,000 and often are lost in storms after a few months. Modelled on the Philippine "payao" raft, the FAD has a drape set below the raft that encourages the growth of micro-organisms on which small fish feed. The small fish attract larger fish, especially tuna, and eventually barracuda and sharks.

We headed toward the FAD, which was easy to spot because of the seagulls that wheeled and dived above the raft, and prepared to do some trolling. The Hartleys have a wooden trolling boom on each side of the hull supported by the cabin roof. Robin said it was time the crew earned their keep and showed us how to fasten "red octopus" lures on the lines attached to the booms and also on two handlines that were coiled under the gunwales amidships. Robin set the boat on a circular course that would bring us close to the FAD but not so close that we risked becoming entangled with it. He gave the signal to toss the lures overboard and the four lines streamed behind us. The first strike came in less than a minute, and it seemed as if we spent the next two hours hauling in the lines, dumping the fish into the ice box and setting the lines out again as fast as we could. In that time we caught 30 kg of fish, mostly skipjack tuna. We used four of the smallest tuna as bait for deep-bottom fishing later in the day. The most exciting moments came when we landed *mahimahi*, beautiful fish with brilliant colors that fade quickly after death.[24] They are also wild fish. We removed the lures from the mouths of all the other fish as soon as they came on board, but not *mahimahi*. I was surprised when Robin wrestled the first *mahimahi* straight into the fish box, line and all; then he slammed the lid down and leaped on top of the fish box, sitting on the lid until the fish grew quiet and it was safe to remove the hook.

The FAD off Araki Island had been in place for about six months and was working well. The seabirds and the fact that we caught about 20 kg of fish in the first 20 minutes of trolling were not the only evidence of the FAD's effectiveness. Many of the fish we pulled in had been attacked by sharks in the short time they were on the line. Robin said there was also a big barracuda who prowled the area and who thought that Fisheries had installed the FAD just for him.

As the sun rose higher, we were catching fewer fish and Robin decided that the excitement of trolling was over. He turned the boat to head for the fishing grounds between Malo and Malekula islands where we would try some bottom fishing. During the hour it took us to reach these grounds, the clouds gave way to Robin's promised fine day. "Now it's time for the hot and boring part, kids!" proclaimed Robin. We stripped off our slickers and, clad in shorts and t-shirts, set to work to find a good place to fish. Locating a bottom of the right depth was not easy, even for Robin, and I could see that a novice village fisherman might soon become discouraged from trying to find new grounds, returning instead to places he knew to have yielded good catches in the past and soon "fishing out" those sites. Three times Robin dropped a lead sinker down 150 meters without reaching bottom, wound it all the way up again, and moved the boat to a new site.

Finally we anchored in about 140 meters of water, baited several hooks on the two handlines coiled on wooden reels—one on each side of the boat more or less amidships—and dropped our lines overboard. Neither the American crew member nor I had much success at first. It was difficult to know when the sinker was in contact with the bottom. And because of the great depth, it was hard to tell when a fish took the bait. Robin taught us to hold the line lightly across our fingertips and to recognize the gentle movement that told of an interested fish more than 100 m below. The trick was then to wait for a second fish to take one of the other hooks, and then pull the line in before a shark took the fish. Two fish, or better still, three fish, made hauling in the line a worthwhile exercise. Dropping and pulling in the line about every ten minutes, I calculated that I had hauled up about 3.36 km of line heavy with fish by the time we quit at about 1 p.m. By that time we had filled the fish box with 70 kg of snapper, poulet, loche, and amberjack tuna in addition to the 30 kg of fish we had caught trolling at dawn.

Returning to port took almost twice as long as our outward bound trip because the Hartley was so heavily laden with fish and the tide was against us. Robin deftly gutted all 100 kg of fish as we headed for home, tossing the guts over the side. Inside the Canal the sea looked tranquil, but when I ineptly dropped a bucket overboard, Robin yelled at me not to reach into water to retrieve it. Sharks were certain to be just below the surface, following the trail of our fish up the Canal.

By the time the boat was cleaned and safely moored off the Fisheries Department offices, I hoped it was time for a shower and a cold beer. All three of us were caked in salt that stung the sunburns we had acquired in the hours that followed the rain. But we still had to sell the fish, so we took the catch to the Santo fish market. The market accepted everything we brought—we kept a yellowfin tuna to turn into *sashimi* for supper and a *mahimahi* to send to my ni-Vanuatu friends on Ambae. Robin earned about $150 from the sale of his day's catch, with prices ranging from $1.80 for poulet to 50 cents for skipjack. Like all Fisheries Department volunteers, Robin was expected to make his boat pay for itself. He used the money earned from fishing to operate, buy gear for, and maintain his boat. He figured that 30 kg of premium fish was enough to break even. Today, even with the most inexperienced of crews, he had done well.

Notes

1. According to the midterm review of the 5 year development plan (1984a:217), Vanuatu expects to take possession of a second patrol vessel in 1987 to assist in fisheries protection, among other things. According to *Pacific Islands Monthly* (August 1987) the patrol boat was to be called "Tugoro," meaning roughly "Protector." A gift from Australia, this ship was expected to cost the Vanuatu government about $180,000 annually to operate, which is more than the revenue the government earned in 1983 from the South Pacific Fishing company (the only Oceanic fishery activity then in Vanuatu).

2. This information comes from James Crossland's report on the Village Fisheries Development Programme prepared for the Fisheries Department (Vanuatu 1984b:1).

3. Listed in Vanuatu's first 5 year plan (Vanuatu 1982:147).

4. In January 1982 a consultant advised that establishing a canning plant would not be economical, because of a lack of local manpower and the high rate of current closings of canneries elsewhere.

5. Fisheries Department Annual Report (Vanuatu 1984:13).

6. Many of the schools were closed at this time because of a teachers' strike, so children were more in evidence in town than usual during weekdays.

7. Crossland (1984b:5).

8. Crossland (1984a:1).

9. The Port Vila facility was designed to have a cold storage capacity equal to three month's supply. The building includes three refrigerated walk-in chill rooms (0°C), two cold stores (120°C), a 600 kg/day blast freezer (-30°C), a 500 kg/day flake ice plant and storage chamber, and a 200 kg/day block ice machine. The Santo market has only one walk in chill room, and a block ice machine with a storage chamber (Crossland 1984a:3–5).

10. The arrangement in 1985 was that Air Melanesiae charged approximately half the usual freight rates so long as Port Vila Fisheries guaranteed payment and accepted any spoilage. These rates for fish were 30 cents/kg within the "inner" zone from Erromanga to Santo, and 60 cents/kg in the outer zone that includes all the islands north of Santo and south of Erromanga. Approximately 23 tons of fish were transported by air between May and December 1983 (Crossland 1984a:11).

11. Allegedly, English observers of this practice coined the slang term "cod's wallop."

12. John Nicholson, personal communication (August 1985).

13. Crossland (1984b:3).

14. ORSTOM stands for the Organisation des Recherches Scientifiques et Techniques d'Outre-Mer. Etelidae comprised 51.5 percent of the catch by weight.

15. Brouard and Grandperrin (1985:21-51).

16. The bone can be removed through the inner side of the skull without impairing the market quality of the fish.

17. This estimate assumes that an Alia-type catamaran using 3 handreels fishes 4 to 5 hours on the outer reef slope per trip, makes 150 trips per year,

and has a mean catch per unit of effort of 3 kg/reel hour (Brouard and Grandperrin 1985:97).

18. Swerdloff (1984:133).

19. In this and subsequent chapters, I have changed the names of the volunteers and islanders with whom I worked to preserve their anonymity. Further, I have altered details concerning peoples' families and places of origin, and I have sought in every way to comply with the standards of ethics for research conducted under the auspices of the Social Sciences and Humanities Council of Canada and the University of Waterloo.

20. Fishing is often regarded as a kind of hunting activity, but never had I heard the analogy made more succinctly. For an example of the view that anthropologically, fishing should be considered as a kind of hunting see Leap (1977).

21. This was one of about 30 boats of the same design, but varying in length from 4 to 6.5 m, that had been built in Santo by 1985 as part of a Fisheries Department project to construct boats for artisanal fishermen. Safety equipment includes a spare 5 hp Seagull outboard motor, lifejackets, flares, a v-sheet, water container, baler and a torch (Crossland 1984b:26). Fishing boats are not equipped with compasses or radios.

22. Fully equipped and insured a 5 m Hartley cost about $6,500 in 1985, but a village fisherman could obtain a Development Bank loan for as much as 40 percent and a grant for as much as 50 percent of the cost of setting up a project with such a boat.

23. Blackburn (1985) provides an assessment of the fishing boats in use in Vanuatu.

24. *Mahimahi* are also known as wahoo or dolphin fish because the shape of their silhouette is similar to that of a dolphin, although they are not related.

6

TRAVELLING HELPERS
AND GRAND DESIGNS

A catamaran, its outboard motor canted above the shallow, tourmaline colored water, floats in Lolowai Bay at the tip of the Longana district of Ambae Island. The fishing boat is nestled along the shoreline, tied to trees fore and aft; the boat is almost invisible in the shadows. It belongs to Jackers Fishing Company, a Village Fisheries Development Project. Most projects in the VFDP consist of just one boat, and the single Alia catamaran is all there is to Jackers. Small as it is, Jackers' power is obvious to the islanders. Jackers drew a Canadian family half-way around the world to spend two years of hard work on the project as cooperants for CUSO.

CUSO Cooperants' Expectations

Cooperants join CUSO for a variety of reasons, but all of them want a chance to find out what it is like to live in another culture. For some, working in Vanuatu is a way to use one's fishing skills to help others. The idea of trading a few Canadian winters for a couple of years in the tropics has a broad appeal. Some join CUSO as a way to break out of a mundane, middle class routine and broaden one's outlook, or as a way to achieve personal growth through giving something of oneself.

CUSO was founded in 1961 in a climate of optimism and idealism. To some of its founders, CUSO, like Canada as a nation, seemed to express a liberal, internationalist position. As Ian Smillie comments in a recent history of the organization, early advocates of the liberal-internationalist view felt that "CUSO would help develop effective, harmonious links between Canada and the Third World, and would contribute to building a more just international order. The organization saw itself as a moderately independent, responsible contributor and participant, both in the development of positive Canadian attitudes towards the world, and in steady, gradual Third World advancement."[1] Others saw CUSO as dominated by CIDA (the Canadian International Development Agency) and felt that CUSO should be more critical of CIDA, of Canada's role as a dependent satellite of the United States, and of the world capitalist system in general.

Smillie argues that neither of these positions has been able to dominate the development of CUSO as an organization over the past 25 years. CUSO, he claims, has preserved a measure of political if not financial independence from CIDA, and has blazed a trail for subsequent NGOs by making its own contacts in the Third World rather than working through Canadian diplomatic channels. This pragmatic orientation is evident in the gradual conversion of CUSO's "good-Samaritan intentions into concrete programs that addressed real needs in Third World countries."[2] Volunteers who serve for two years, earning about four or five thousand dollars a year, have become the heart of CUSO's programs.

Individuals who volunteer to work with CUSO attend pre-orientation, predeparture orientation, and in-country orientation sessions to prepare for the experience of serving overseas. They learn that they are expected "to increase their understanding of the root causes of inequitable development in all countries of the world."[3] They learn that one of CUSO's major goals is to free "people, not just from constraints of poverty, hunger, and disease, but also from constraints which inhibit a person's control over his [or her] destiny, the pursuit of dignity and social equality."[4] They are prepared for the medical problems they may encounter and they are made aware of some of the difficulties of cross-cultural communication that they may find in their new jobs. But none of the CUSO cooperants I talked to felt that these orientation sessions could really prepare them for what it is like to work in fisheries development in Vanuatu.

Toward sundown, the CUSO cooperants who are passing through or working in Port Vila tend to gather at the Rossi Hotel to share a few beers. Watching the sun set and the lights come on in the island resort across the harbour, they often comment on the contrast between these surroundings and what they had thought they would find in Vanuatu.

One CUSO couple expected to serve two years in Papua New Guinea. When they were told that the Papua New Guinea project had fallen through and that they would instead be posted to Vanuatu, the couple's response was "What country is Vanuatu the capital of?" At first, like many CUSO couples, they were unhappy in Port Vila. The cosmopolitan amenities that make Port Vila seem like paradise to anthropologists who come to town from the outer islands make the town a disappointment for CUSO cooperants who must live there. For a young couple eager to try their hand at living in an isolated fishing village, the prospect of spending two years in a four-bedroom split-level house next door to a Minister in the Vanuatu government was disconcerting. "We had clear expectations about being able to help ni-Vanuatu," one volunteer remembered, "But in Port Vila it was difficult even to meet any." Port Vila is not part of the Third World, according to CUSO volunteers, and the Third World is where they thought they were going.[5]

In contrast to Port Vila, the outer islands have a special attraction, an authenticity more in keeping with volunteers' expectations. One couple liked to tell of their arrival at the remote island that was to be their home. They travelled slowly from Port Vila in a small fishing boat heavily laden with their household effects. Night had fallen by the time they sighted the island, a long dark silhouette in the moonlit sea. Way out in the distance a man in a lone canoe was fishing. The scene was a rare glimpse of a Vanuatu that perfectly fulfilled the Canadian imagination of the place.

In general, volunteers have been uncertain about what to expect concerning small-scale fishing in Vanuatu, although they are experienced fishermen under Canadian conditions. Often, CUSO volunteers come to Vanuatu with a conviction that "small is better," a predisposition to encourage fishing for subsistence at the village level, and an antipathy to "cargo"—that is, to using expensive technology or equipment to solve problems. They are unaware that the fish they catch in the outer islands may exceed local demand and be sold to the Port Vila fish market. They may even be unaware that the fish they catch will be sold at all.

One young fisherman told me that he wrote in his journal before leaving Vancouver for Vanuatu, "I'm not sure exactly what we're supposed to be doing down there. I'm not sure if we're supposed to be selling the fish or just giving it away to help the people in the villages." His partner added that they were disillusioned to discover they had come to a country that wasn't a "needy" country. She laughed as she told me "We really thought that we would come in after a day's fishing and there would be people with bloated bellies waiting on the beach for the catch."

There are times, especially during holidays, when a volunteer can be gratified by local enthusiasm for fresh fish. One volunteer recounted the pleasure of coming ashore at Easter time on Pentecost Island with about 90 kg of fresh fish. "I couldn't get ashore in my dinghy," he beamed, "because people were wading out into the water to grab the fish." But overall, volunteers soon learn, the pace of life in the islands is slower and more low key than they could have thought possible back in Canada. Local people like to eat fish and some of them like to catch fish, but they do both on a very small scale by Canadian standards. Fisheries cooperants learn, as the CUSO staff emphasizes during the orientation sessions, that patience is the most important thing a volunteer can take to a developing country, and that it is impossible to take enough.

No Grand Designs:
VFDP's Expectations of Volunteers

The first six months of a volunteer's service with the Village Fisheries Development Program (VFDP) are a crucial period for establishing rapport, not only with the local people but with the Fisheries Department. When I was in Vanuatu in 1985, I spoke with the manager of the VFDP, David Shepherd, about his expectations concerning volunteers. The English manager's curly black hair showed signs of gray, but his otherwise youthful appearance made it easy to believe that he, too, had worked as a volunteer. David served with VSO, the English volunteer organization, during the mid-1970s in the Turks and Caicos Islands. Later he was involved in fisheries development in Papua New Guinea. Back in England, Shepherd became a self-employed fish marketer; although he enjoyed being his own boss, he found the work boring. He was pleased when he had the chance to come to Vanuatu because, as far as fisheries development was concerned, the country "hadn't already been messed up by anyone else."[6]

With a smile, David Shepherd styled himself as "not a very easy bloke to work for." He enjoyed that image. He liked "his" volunteers to be independent so that he could maintain what he called a "hands-off" management style. Yet volunteers must learn not to be too independent. They were supposed to keep David informed so that little problems didn't accumulate and become big ones, yet they shouldn't "waste his time with trivia." They should be managers in the sense that if called upon they should be capable of establishing a permanent fishing operation and running it on a day to day basis. While the volunteers were expected to be resourceful and self-reliant, David was wary of those with "grand designs" for changing the way a project is implemented in the islands.

During their first six months in Vanuatu, Shepherd has often found it difficult to keep volunteers on "the straight and narrow." Shepherd commented to me, "This is when they get all the great ideas, grand designs. There is this tendency to think that money is unlimited whereas we're on a fairly tight budget. It's not that bad, actually; I just don't like to see it wasted. I've seen it all before with the grand schemes and great designs."

The first quality that the manager looked for in a successful VFDP volunteer was an ability to establish a rapport with the local people. He liked them to have a "reasonable standard of education," because poor bookkeeping skills are one of the most frequent reasons that a project fails. A volunteer should have a "reasonable mechanical skill—to be able to fix the engine and keep it going. And lastly, they require a reasonable fishing skill, but that's very much the lowest priority because the fishing is simple, otherwise we wouldn't be putting it in."

In many of the VFDP projects, everything has been new and untested—the volunteer, the village fishermen, the equipment. So Shepherd has tended to tie new volunteers to particular projects for the first 6 or 8 months by placing them in their island posting without a boat during this "shakedown" period. "They don't get a boat before," he explains, "So they won't go off and leave the project floundering." Once the volunteer settled into his posting and the fishing project he came to oversee was well underway, he might receive a small fishing boat to use for exploring new fishing grounds, teaching other islanders, and so on. Until then, the only way the volunteer could get out on the water is in the fishing boat belonging to the ni-Vanuatu project which, in Shepherd's estimation, the volunteer came to manage.

The VFDP manager's own words summarize his expectations of volunteers as he choses to present them to me: "The ones who do best are the ones who get on with the local people, who drink kava[7] with them, who can sit down and talk with them, and who learn Bislama fluently. I respect a certain amount of independence, but I'm very simple minded: the idea is to leave behind a *permanent fishing business*. That's my criterion of success: if it's permanent, it's successful. And however big it is, if it's not permanent, you're not successful. So I'd prefer to see [the volunteers] keep it very low key so that it will continue on after they leave. This is where I think we've had some trouble with a couple of volunteers who have had grand designs. I'm not into grand designs."

A Travelling Helper in Lolowai Bay

One of the central assumptions underlying cooperants' expectations about their posts in Vanuatu is that they will work themselves out of a job. Ideally, they transfer their skills to local people who can then take over from the volunteer at the end of two years. But this ideal is hard for some volunteers to carry out in practice because of their own temperaments and because of the situations in which they find themselves. One who, in the eyes of other cooperants, succeeded particularly well in achieving this goal was the village fisheries advisor (VFA) posted to Lolowai on Ambae from 1983 to 1985.

In the words of a fellow cooperant, the VFA whom I shall call Tom Daniels and was a travelling helper: "At our CUSO orientation in Ottawa they told us, 'You're going to put yourself out of a job.' And I thought, 'Yeah, that's what's supposed to happen, that's the right idea. But you get here and find not everybody's working that way. *Some are. Like I think Tom was really good in the way he was just a travelling helper* (my emphasis)."

Tom Daniels arrived in Vanuatu on the last day of July, 1983. He came from a fishing village in eastern Canada with his wife, whom I shall call Mary, and a daughter of elementary school age. Mary and Tom were posted to Lolowai Bay on Ambae, where Tom was to serve as a Village Fisheries Advisor and Mary, like other "non-working" spouses in CUSO, was expected to help her husband or create her own job in the community. They settled in Torgil, an Anglican girls' boarding school that had been converted to a training college for catechists.

I knew Torgil well. Until the recent establishment of the local government headquarters at Saraitamata on the road between Torgil and Longana, the school was the first sign of "town" that Bill and I encountered on rare trips into Lolowai from our village to collect the mail. For me, the sight of Torgil's mature fruit trees—mango, mandarin, avocado—and raised wooden houses wrapped with verandas in the best colonial style still evokes the lively and disciplined community of island schoolgirls in blue skirts and white blouses that was Torgil as we first saw it at Christmastime in 1969. But by the time the Daniels arrived in 1983, Torgil was a collection of rundown, partly abandoned, institutional buildings set on the grassy slope of an ancient volcano open to the sea.

From Saraitamata, the local government headquarters on the edge of Longana, the dirt road winds along the side of the Torgil crater. Then in a hairpin turn the road crests the lip of that crater and bends back to overlook a second spatter cone. Walking on that road, I used to pause just at the crest between the two craters to catch my breath, enjoy the breeze that blew there even when the valleys below were hot and still, and admire the view. Lolowai is the centerpiece of the second crater. Its azure bay is picturesque evidence for the merging of blue and green in the vocabularies of Melanesian languages. The entrance to the bay is a narrow passage between the submerged crater lip and a sea cliff, but the bay itself is deep and sheltered from all but the north wind. Lolowai Bay provides the safest anchorage on Ambae and is the only harbor available to Longana people. Beyond the bay is yet another crater wall. The road climbs over the rim into a third volcanic valley where Vureas High School is located. This trinity of ancient spatter cones comprises what began as an Anglican mission, grew to be the Vanuatu headquarters of the Diocese of Melanesia, and has become a town.

About 200 people live between Saraitamata and Vureas High School, a distance of about 3 km. Some Ambae and Maevo people live in the area, but most of the Lolowai residents are Pentecost islanders who came to Ambae because of the mission. Overall, residents are relatively well-educated; most are salaried and used to working at full-time jobs. A handful of expatriates are usually in residence in the area, working as teachers or for the government. The settlement retains a mission atmosphere; church leaders and elected Pentecost chiefs run the community. While Lolowai is a town in terms of its size and amenities, it operates at a pace that is considerably slower than Port Vila or even Santo. Population density is low. Communication within the area is neither swift nor sure. All in all, life in Lolowai would not seem urban to a visitor from outside Vanuatu.

But the Saraitamata to Vureas area provides a number of services not available elsewhere in east Ambae. There is an agricultural extension office, a police station, a post office, a 20 bed hospital with a medical officer and nursing staff, a bank, bakery, joinery, mission school and two stores. There is a telephone at the Lolowai post office and at Saraitamata; the solar-powered telephones are unreliable in cloudy weather. When they are operating, the telephones are heavily used for calls to other islands rather than for communication between Lolowai and Saraitamata. The Longana airfield is about 4 km from Lolowai; there are flights to and from Santo six days a week. Ambaebulu, a residential primary school is located in Longana about 2 km from Lolowai. Small diesel and gasoline generators supply the Lolowai area with electricity for three hours in the evening (until about 9 p.m.).

Lack of a reliable water supply and adequate land suitable for gardening are the major deficiencies of community life. Fresh meat is often available from the Vureas High School's abattoir, but fresh vegetables are sometimes impossible to obtain. There is no fresh produce market.

In general, Lolowai residents have had little fresh fish to eat. Some people dive or fish from canoes as a recreational activity, but there was no regular fishing activity prior to the VFDP. Fear of fish poisoning was a damper on peoples' enthusiasm for eating fish.

Ciguatera fish poisoning cases were not uncommon at the Lolowai hospital. Ciguatera poisoning is caused by micro-organisms on which certain species of fish feed some of the time. Damage to a reef, such as blasting a channel, causes the micro-organism to proliferate. Ciguatera poisoning affects the nervous system and can cause severe pains in the limbs as well as itching that linger for days or even weeks. Deep water snappers and poulet fish are free from ciguatera. But only the crews of mission or cargo ships had access to safer deep water species, and they did not always choose their fish well. I remember one occasion when the entire crew of the Anglican mission ship, *Southern Cross*, were sick in hospital with fish poisoning.

When Tom arrived, there were no fishing projects operating in the area although the Jackers project was in the planning stage. Except for the experience gained when a team from the South Pacific Commission came to Lolowai and trained local people, no one was familiar with handlining techniques to catch the safe, deep water fish.

Torgil became home to the Daniels for two years, but, like many CUSO volunteers, they found that their new life in Vanuatu wasn't quite what they had expected. First, Tom and Mary had expected to live in a house that was to be built by the members of Jackers Fishing Company. Second, Tom had expected to serve as an advisor, not only to Jackers but to other fledgling projects that might be encouraged in the area; it was important to him to be an advisor, not a manager. Within the first three months, Tom found that the expectations of the Fisheries Department and of Jackers Fishing Company were very different from his own.

The house into which he had planned to settle on the shores of Lolowai Bay did not exist when the Daniels arrived. Tom and Mary found that if they wanted the house constructed, they would have to do much of the work themselves because of an apparent lack of interest on the part of the islanders who formed the Jackers company. So Tom spent his first two months on Ambae building the house that he had thought was a precondition for his arrival.

This is not unusual. Suitable housing is a prerequisite that CUSO requires of islanders before agreeing to post a cooperant. But a promise to build a house is not the same as a completed building, and CUSO volunteers find that carpentry skills are an asset, for their first task is often to build their homes.

Anthropologists are not exempt from this problem of homelessness. Construction of our bamboo house in Waileni did not begin until after we arrived in Longana. We were disappointed, as Tom and Mary must have been, for we had come from Canada with our then six-year-old son expecting to move right in to the new home for which we had planned so carefully. Unlike Tom and Mary, we had the advantage of knowing the people and the language; the villagers seemed to like us and to be in favor of building our house. Bill's adoptive father had urged us to build the house on his land and had selected the site. We sent a simple, but detailed description of the kind of house we wanted. Moreover, we had sent the money to pay for the house's construction months ahead of time. But, as Tom and Mary found in Lolowai, when we arrived weary after the long journey from Canada, our child disoriented and cranky, all our possessions in suitcases, there was no house.

It takes North Americans a long time to understand that from the villagers' viewpoint it is commonsensical not to build the house until after the occupants arrive. How could they be sure we would really come until they saw us? How could they be sure we would like what we saw if they went ahead and built the house before our arrival? If this was how villagers felt about building a house for us, whom they knew, consider how much more reluctant they would be to build a house for CUSO cooperants who were complete strangers.

Tom was happy to help with the construction of the house, but resisted fulfilling the fishing company's expectation that he take over the entire task, which he thought should be their responsibility not his own. In the end, the Daniels never lived in the new house. Instead, they remained at Torgil and the fisheries house became sleeping quarters for the Jackers crew. There was an ongoing dispute over the house throughout Tom's two years in Ambae. From the point of view of the Fisheries Department the house was a prerequisite for the fishing project and belonged to the department. If Jackers used it for their crew, the fishing project must pay Tom's rent for the Torgil house. But from the point of view of Jackers' manager, the new house belonged to the islanders involved in the company not to the Fisheries Department, and Tom's rent was not Jackers' responsibility.

Tom felt that instead of building the house his time should have been spent exploring new fishing grounds, trying out techniques that were new to him, and teaching islanders. But like other fisheries volunteers in their first months of service, Tom had not been given a boat to use for his work, and the fishing boat for the Jackers project had not yet arrived.

Tom resisted what he saw as a managerial role in the fishing project because this violated his purpose in coming to Vanuatu. He wanted to transfer his skills to islanders, to work himself out of a job. As the other cooperants recognized, Tom did want to be a travelling helper;

but his job threatened to become one that is more familiar to islanders, that of expatriate manager.

For Mary, whose expectations seem to have been less clear-cut because she had no specific job awaiting her, the first few months on Ambae were spent making a place for herself and her family. She fixed up an old house on the Torgil campus, gave it a good cleaning and built shelves and cupboards. She began teaching their daughter using Canadian correspondence course materials, although the child also attended the local primary school. She helped Tom mix and pour cement for the fisheries house; nearby, she planted a vegetable garden. Soon Mary had involved herself in the local school where she began to play her guitar, sing to the children and tell them stories with the help of her hand puppet. She looked forward to becoming more involved with the schoolchildren and felt fairly confident about the work she was doing.

For the Daniels' daughter, the atmosphere of the the Torgil Training Center was like summer camp. Because she was a child, her ni-Vanuatu neighbors interacted with her in a more relaxed, informal way than with her parents, and she was able to experience day to day life on Ambae in a way that Tom and Mary could not. She spent hours each day in the houses of her new friends. She learned traditional string games and other games that may once have come from missionaries' children such as *gon vano, gon mai* (go away, come here) which is a form of hide-and-seek. She came home smelling of hearth smoke and breadfruit, telling traditional tales, and expressing her own ideas about family life in the islands.

Notes

1. Smillie (1985:352).

2. Ibid., 355.

3. A quotation from the CUSO Development Charter used in the CUSO-Vanuatu termination report questionnaire.

4. Ibid.

5. Quotations from cooperants and ni-Vanuatu throughout this book come either from transcripts of tape recorded interviews (translated from Bislama, in the case of ni-Vanuatu) or from detailed notes made during conversations. I have attempted to preserve the anonymity of those who talked to me by mingling the personal characteristics of individuals, using pseudonyms, and changing the locations of some events.

6. This sentiment was one I also heard expressed in the 1970s by colonial officials who had come to Vanuatu from Africa.

7. Kava is a drink made from the roots of a pepper plant (*Piper Methysticum*) that men consumed traditionally in Vanuatu and that has become increasingly popular in recent years as a substitute, and sometimes a

supplement, for alcoholic beverages. Kava has mildly narcotic properties, has a customary reputation as a health tonic that recently received pharmacological support, has what most drinkers regard as a terrible taste, and creates a pleasant state of mental and physical relaxation. (For more on kava see Brunton 1979, Lindstrom 1987, and Philibert 1986.

Photographs

The white sand of Port Olry's sheltered beach (*left*), St. Peter's Star, an Alia catamaran belonging to Jackers Fishing Company, moored in Lolowai Bay, Ambae (*below*)

A good day's catch trolling
and deep water handlining
(*right*), Pascaline (research
assistant for the study), the
author, and her children
(Sean and Channing) walk
along Port Olry beach
(*below*)

Outrigger canoe and dinghy equipped for deep water fishing, Port Olry

7

CONSUMING DEVELOPMENT IN LONGANA

Jackers Fishing Company, owner of the catamaran moored in Lolowai Bay, gave CUSO a reason to place a cooperant family there and gave the Fisheries Department one more VFDP project to add to its growing list. The project also gave Longanans cause to wonder. Is this what they should expect of development? Who is it for?

This chapter tells a story of expectations that go beyond those held by the CUSO cooperants and the Fisheries Department to include the variety of expectations held by those involved in the fishing project and by other Longana people. The contrasts between these various expectations highlight different assumptions, objectives, and ways of doing things. These contrasting expectations also draw attention to broader issues in development. Who benefits from projects such as the VFDP? Who is *expected* to benefit from these projects? What are the social and economic costs of such projects? The best answers to these questions may be another series of queries, hard ones that we must ask ourselves about the meaning of development and about who needs it.

What Does Development Mean in Longana?

When I first visited Longana in 1969, I found that people cared a great deal about carrying some of their customary past forward into the future. Traditions involving pigs and mats, rank-taking in the graded society, ways of settling conflict and treating others with respect, all were important to maintain. But Longanans were eager to leave other aspects of their past way of life behind. Cannibalism ended along with warfare in the 1930s. Christianity became deeply rooted in the culture. Islanders came to rely on Western forms of education and health care, without losing touch with traditional ways of teaching and healing.[1] Customary techniques for hurting are believed also to have survived; they may yet cause illness and even death.

Swidden horticulture provides Longanans with subsistence. This means that they clear the land by slashing and burning the brush, then cultivate a garden for a year or so before moving on to a new plot. Except when a major clearing operation is necessary, each residential segment[2] (consisting of a single household or a few closely related households) works separately. The men do much of the heavy work of clearing the undergrowth and the women do much of the weeding, but there is no absolute division of labor in the garden. Households most often go together to their gardens and spend the day there, husbands, wives, and children working together. Most crops such as yams are harvested at the end of the first growing season, but the gardeners return to the plot in the second year to harvest bananas. Subsequently, the land is allowed to lie fallow for about five years.

Like most ni-Vanuatu, Longanans are involved in both subsistence production and cash-cropping.[3] While they have retained control over their own land, they have no influence over the price they receive for their copra or over most other terms of trade. They have participated as simple commodity producers in the market economy since they began their own small coconut plantations in the 1930s and '40s. Most local people planted coconuts in their stone-fenced gardens so that the coconut palms remained and grew after the food crops were harvested. Because coconut palms bear fruit for as much as 75 years, planting land in coconuts effectively took it out of circulation for subsistence, so landholding took on a new significance. People with use-rights to a land parcel could plant food gardens there, but only those individuals with rights as landholders could plant coconuts.

The customary system of land tenure remains in practice, supported by the stipulation in the Vanuatu Constitution that all land belongs to the customary owners. In Longana, the practice is for land to be held by males individually or as a set of brothers. Occasionally a woman may be in charge of a parcel of land, usually as a way of holding a place for her son. Land passes from fathers to sons, or is passed matrilineally between men. Typically, a man inherits some land from his mother's brother and some from his own father. Landholding, especially since the introduction of cash-cropping, is subject to frequent and prolonged disputes, and knowledge of the land—historically and spatially—is crucial to making an effective claim to it. By and large, transmission of control over land occurs in the course of the hundred-day-long cycle of funerary feasts. Through these feasts, through appropriation in the days of warfare, and through knowledge of past events and relationships, a few Longana men have been able to acquire considerably more land than others.[4]

The title of another of my books, *Masters of Tradition* (1987), refers to those men who use traditional pathways of knowledge and exchange to gain unprecedented wealth through landholdings. In 1978, these men were 5 percent of Longanan landholders. They controlled 31 percent of the land under coconuts and earned incomes from copra sales that were more than four times greater than the average. That is, they earned incomes of about $9,500 per year while other landholding units averaged about $2,300.

So far, everyone has access to enough coconuts on their own or their relatives' land to make at least a few hundred dollars a year from copra. Most producers make copra only when they need cash, which they require in small amounts. Coconut palms tolerate periods of neglect fairly well;[5] cash-cropping, then, need not be a full-time activity. This suits Longanans because most of them prefer not to make copra week in and week out. They dislike the routine and the heavy labor involved in producing copra as a business. Moreover, they have alternative demands on their labor. Households produce not only for subsistence and to earn cash, but also for traditional kinds of exchange (tusked pigs, mats, services) that ensure the social security and the reproduction of the domestic group.[6]

There are signs of increasing social differentiation in Longana. Wealthier landholders employ fellow islanders as wage laborers. But differentiation has not proceeded very far for several reasons. First, tradition has masked new forms of inequality, making wealthy landholders appear to be nothing more than exemplars of a customary model of success. Second, redistribution of wealth in the form of pigs contributed to graded society ceremonies, mats given at weddings, and both money and business opportunities given to kinsmen have helped to level income inequalities. Third, there have been few ways for the rich to get richer in Longana. Development projects and investment opportunities were rare before independence and are only beginning now to reach the rural areas.[7]

The Village Fisheries Development Program has provided a new kind of small-business activity, branching out beyond the small stores and truck-taxis that have supplemented copra incomes for Longana entrepreneurs. For most islanders, however, copra production has remained intermittent and consumption oriented (in the sense of working toward a target income); gardening and customary exchange continue to be important alternative ways to allocate their labor. In other words, for many years Longanans have had one foot somewhat tentatively in the capitalist marketplace and the other squarely in a traditional lifestyle based on values and relationships that are very different from those underlying a capitalist way of life.

By the time of my fieldwork in 1982, Longanans had more cement houses, trucks, generators for electric light, water tanks, and radios than ever before. By 1985, there was even a video cassette recorder in the district; the first videotape ever shown in the village where we lived was a documentary on the sinking of the Greenpeace ship *Rainbow Warrior* in New Zealand. Longana has changed. Is it developing?

"Development" is a problematic term, but it is one that the Longana people themselves use. Locally, development ("devlopmen" in Bislama) means "lifting the place up"—raising standards, improving the place—and Longanans have been involved in schemes to achieve this goal since long before I first met them. There is a fine difference between development, which local people regard as improving conditions for a place or community of people, and business, which is intended to bring prosperity to an individual or a company, often composed of relatives. Development, then, can introduce changes that do not generate income; development is seen to be a matter of digging latrines and forming school committees as well as establishing fishing projects.

Projects that *do* generate income are often the subject of local controversy. Private entrepreneurs who succeed in making a profit generally are subject to redistributive demands from their kinsmen,[8] and successful businessmen often inspire jealousy. Similarly, recipients of income generating development projects may be seen as personally profiting rather than helping their community.

This view is not restricted to local people who feel that their lives, not just those of a few fortunate individuals, should be improved by the presence of a development project in the area. As development workers, expatriate volunteers in Vanuatu wonder what they should expect of development: Is it for individuals or communities? Should development benefit those whose relative affluence demonstrates their aptitude as entrepreneurs? Or should projects such as those in the VFDP assist poorer people?

To Do Things on My Own:
Expectations of the Jackers's Skipper

Jackers Fishing Company was Silas Bageo's idea. I first met Silas in 1969, when he was the radio operator for the Diocese of Melanesia. He worked at Lolowai, sending and receiving the messages that kept the mission in touch with Santo and Port Vila. I remember Silas as an outspoken young man. Then 20 years old, he was almost six feet tall, slim and angular, with coppery skin, prominent brown eyes, hair cut in an Afro, and a direct gaze that contrasted with the shyness of many of his peers. Even then, Silas wanted to accomplish things; he wanted to show others, islanders and outsiders alike, that he could achieve things on his own. Ironically, community development provided a way for Silas to achieve his individual goals.

Silas had gone to work for the Diocese of Melanesia after he graduated from Class 8 at the local school. He rode a Honda motorcycle to work from his home in the village of Lovonda, about 10 km from Lolowai. Silas left the job after three years because, he told me, "the salary was very poor. The Diocese only paid me $14 a month and I had to run my motorbike to get down to work. It just wasn't worth it."

When Silas quit his job and moved back to Lovonda, Fr. Walter Lini, then a parish priest, was living in the village. In Lovonda, Fr. Walter embarked on the political career that led him to become Prime Minister. His political commitment had both a national and a local focus. He became involved in founding the New Hebrides Cultural Association, which evolved into the Vanuaaku Pati, but he also began to think about community development. Fr. Walter made plans to start the Longana Peoples' Center in the village of Lovonda. Silas worked with him, and in March 1974, Fr. Walter sent Silas to Papua New Guinea for a year-long course in community development. Shortly after Silas had completed this course and returned to Lovonda, he was sent to Fiji to attend another course, this time on "youth management."

Already, Silas had been identified as what might be called a consumer of development. It was not his own idea to attend the courses in New Guinea or Fiji. Regarding the Fiji course, he said, "I went because somebody wanted me, I think it was the government, wanted me to go." He welcomed this identity because it gave him access to a world of projects and grants through which he could realize his personal ambitions. But he found that his experiences with community development could cost him friends. The Fiji course lasted for three months. Upon his return to Lovonda, Silas took charge of the Longana Peoples' Center and began to put what he had learned about community development into practice. But Silas had a hot temper, and his new job did not go smoothly. In his words, "After I came back [from Fiji] I worked for a short time at the center. But you know how Melanesian people are. Well, you know how they often get jealous of somebody who seems to be making a lot of money. This was especially true of the committee [in charge] of the Longana Peoples' Center. [The committee members] criticized me for working very little and making a great deal of money. I got tired of hearing all of these complaints and I stopped working there."

In 1976, Silas was once again involved in the Longana Peoples' Centre where he worked for about a year with a young Australian who had come to Ambae to introduce "appropriate technology" through such projects as leather tanning and sandal making. But again, there was a falling out, this time with the expatriate. Silas started to install a radio antenna at the center. The Australian advisor told Silas that he was going about the installation the wrong way. Silas says, "We argued over this. I got angry because I thought I knew what I was doing. I had a lot of experience with radios when I worked with the Diocese of Melanesia. [The Australian] spoke harshly with me and I didn't want to work with him any longer."

Silas began to make plans for a project in which he could be his own boss. "I thought about what I wanted to do. I wanted to make something, to accomplish something. I didn't want to just hang around and amount to nothing." He began to make copra regularly in order to buy a truck that he could then use as a taxi to make money.

For Silas, it didn't matter what the project was so long as it was his own. I asked him to explain why he was so interested in having some sort of development project in the late 1970s. "I wanted to do a project on my own because the committee members were saying that I had stolen money, that I had taken too much money from the Center," he told me. The line between jealousy and an accusation of theft is a fine one in Longana; to Silas it had seemed that others were just jealous, but as his comment reveals, to members of the committee he seemed guilty of theft. Silas continued, "I felt that if I did something like [start a project], people would see that I had enough wherewithal to do things on my own. That it would clear my name of the criticisms that people had been levelling at me."

Silas prepared to apply to the Development Bank for a loan with which to buy a truck. He married a local woman and together they made copra on both Silas's father's land and on her father's land. He saved some money toward a downpayment for the truck and used part of the copra income to start a small business selling such items as tinned fish to local people. He also repaired an old oven and organized a small bread-making operation in Lovonda. Silas's brother decided to join in the truck venture and the money the two households saved went into a bank account in the brother's name. By 1981, there was $1,000 in the account.

But Silas began to change his mind about the wisdom of buying a truck when he learned about the Village Fisheries Development Program. He attended a brief training course at Lolowai run by the

South Pacific Commission. Silas paid attention to what the leaders of the training course said about the grants that were available to supplement Development Bank loans for small fishing projects. Compared to buying a truck, Silas learned, a fishing boat was relatively inexpensive. "So the idea of a truck didn't seem so attractive any more, and anyway a lot of people had trucks already," Silas told me, "My thinking began to change. I thought, 'Well, fishing is a pretty good business!' "

Silas had little experience as a fisherman. He says that his father knew a lot about fishing and taught him to fish. Although Silas told me that he was a person who liked to fish, he had never fished with a net. He had never left the shore to fish in a canoe. As a child, he said, he and his friends would stand on a rock at the water's edge and toss a hook and line into the sea or attempt to spear small fish from the shore.

One reason that Silas gave for wanting to start a fishing company is commonly cited by ni-Vanuatu who enter into development projects. As Silas expressed it, "I thought, well, there are a lot of young boys around here who leave school and can't find employment. It would be good if these boys could go fishing and make a little money." Although Silas sought to achieve recognition for his personal accomplishments, he realized the cultural correctness of doing so in a way that involved participation from the community at large. Since making friends with Fr. Walter Lini in the early 1970s, Silas had remained involved with the Vanuaaku Pati. He attended the party commissars' congresses and, in the 1980s, served as an elected representative to the Ambae-Maevo Local Government.

In short, Silas Bageo saw himself as a community-minded man who wanted to do things for himself. A fishing project provided him with an opportunity that was consistent with his self image and within his financial means. When he learned that a fishing project would amount to half the cost of a truck, he says he "jumped right over to the fishing project."

In October 1981, Silas wrote to the Fisheries Department using the Longana Peoples' Center as his return address. He had ready the $1,000 personal contribution needed to acquire an Alia catamaran for the proposed fishing project, and he hoped that he could take delivery of the boat in January 1982. The Director of Fisheries replied that the establishment of the Village Fisheries Development Program was moving more slowly than anticipated, but that he hoped to start Silas's project as soon as possible in 1982.

By November 1982, Silas's situation had changed in two ways that were important financially and semantically. First, the money for his personal contribution to the fishing project had "disappeared" from his brother's bank account. Silas enlisted his brothers, his father-in-law, and a handful of other relatives to begin raising the money again. They made an acronym of their initials, "Jackers," which became the name of the fishing company. Second, Silas's father died, leaving his sons some money which Silas, as the oldest son, put toward the fishing project. Although the loss of the original money angered Silas and delayed the project, he and his brothers had no difficulty coming up with a second $1,000 by the end of 1982. Silas decided to name the long-awaited catamaran after his father, Peter.

St. Peter's Star: The Story
of a VFDP Fishing Project, 1983–85

"At first I chose the name 'Peter's Star' for the boat," Silas explained, "The star means something like a dream. We don't think we can reach it, but . . . And the more I thought about the name, the better it seemed because St. Peter had been a fisherman. So I called it 'St. Peter's Star.' " This statement struck me as a distilled expression of the Melanesian success model discussed in Chapter 3, in which those whose success was least expected—i.e, those who "don't think they can reach it, but . . ."—are those whose achievement is most socially esteemed.

Silas Bageo and Tom Daniels took delivery of St. Peter's Star in late November 1983. With two crew members, they spent a week at the Fisheries Department in Santo preparing the Alia catamaran, engines, fishing gear and safety equipment for the eight-hour crossing to Lolowai.

Alia catamarans were the first fishing boats used in the VFDP. These are 8.5 m FAO designed, wooden boats with twin hulls, a 25 hp outboard motor, and four handreels. The Fisheries Department has been phasing out the Alia boats, preferring to supply projects with smaller Hartley monohulls that are more fuel efficient, can operate effectively with fewer fishermen, and handle better under rough sea conditions. By the time Silas and Tom outfitted St. Peter's Star other projects were beginning to use Hartley boats, but Silas had trained on an Alia during his SPC course, and he was happy with the boat. "We got the Alia," Silas told me, "because the boat had been promised to us for a long time. $1,000 meant an Alia and so I worked hard to earn $1,000."[9]

The cost of setting up the Jackers Fishing Company was $10,000. The boat itself cost $6,400. Equipping the boat with motors and gear cost $2,600. Other expenses and working capital made up the balance of the setting-up costs. Silas contributed the $1,000 he and other members of the company had raised. The project received a grant from the Economic Development Fund for $5,000, and a Development Bank loan covered the remaining $4,000. Silas was surprised that all he had to do to obtain the loan was to fill out a simple, single page application.

By the time St. Peter's Star set out on its maiden voyage to Ambae, Tom had been in Lolowai for about two and a half months. Initially, Tom had been enthusiastic about working with Silas, but disenchantment soon set in, partly because the fishermen were contributing so little to the construction of the fisheries house.

Lack of interest in the house seemed indicative of more serious problems with fisheries development. It seemed too easy for someone like Silas, who could raise $1,000 twice and knew how to approach the government, to get fishing projects. Tom favored smaller projects that used less imported materials and that would benefit those with the greatest need. Smaller projects would make better use of the fish resource, the size of which was not well-established; and smaller projects would be more likely to benefit local people instead of enriching the international producers of engines, fuel, etc. Self-reliance for Vanuatu should continue to be a major objective of the VFDP, and, in Tom's view, the goal of self-reliance should include becoming less dependent on foreign aid. Islanders interested in fishing should be encouraged to adapt their canoes and to gain fishing experience without incurring debts or using grants from aid donors.

Tom had communicated his doubts about whether the VFDP was able to achieve its objectives in letters and telephone calls to the manager, David Shepherd, who saw in Tom's dissatisfaction the ominous beginnings of a "grand design." While Tom wondered, "Are $5,000 loans and 28 foot outboard motors really the next step from outrigger canoes?" David urged him to get on with his work and admonished Tom that he had not "yet grasped some of the basic tenets of working in a developing country."

The divergence between David's and Tom's assumptions about the purpose of fisheries development is highlighted in a statement David made that "canoe fishing will be important but it will always be a part-time activity. If we want people to have a full-time job then they must be able to fish more frequently than would be possible from canoes." For Tom, the point of fisheries development was not to give people full-time jobs. He asked David for a boat of his own so that he could help those local fishermen outside of Jackers's project who asked for his assistance.

For his part, Silas was keen on retaining control over the Jackers project and over Tom's services, but less enthusiastic about fishing as a full-time job. To set an example for the crew and to have the pleasure of testing the new boat, Silas served as captain of St. Peter's Star for the first two months of the project. In February, Silas allowed a "brother" (his father's brother's son) to replace him as captain. Silas himself did not fish again until late June. Under the new captain catches declined from an average of about $400/mo for the first four months of the project's operation to only $52 in April.

Early problems for the Jackers Company included difficulties catching bait and failure to sell less-desirable species. Shark accounted for a large portion of early catches; Ambae women will not eat shark for fear that their babies will be born dead. Shark is not a very popular eating fish even among islanders who have no tabu about its consumption. The Fisheries Department gave advice regarding trolling techniques to improve catches of tuna for bait. Tom refined techniques for catching premium species, and gradually the mixture of fish caught bottom fishing included more commercial species.

But advice from the Fisheries Department and practice on the part of the VFA were not the only solutions offered to Jackers. By the end of its first six months of operation, Jackers had a kerosene freezer installed in the fisheries house where the crew slept at Lolowai. The project's gross sales for this period were only $1750, or less than $300 per month. About 340 kg of Jackers' catch had failed to sell during the project's first six months. Most of the unsold fish was unpopular shark and oilfish, which would not have been priced as high as the $1/kg charged for other deep-bottom species, so it is safe to say that the unsold kilograms represented less than $340 in foregone sales. Not only is $340 a lot less than the price of a freezer (about $1700), it seems unlikely that frozen shark and oilfish would find eventual buyers if there was little interest in the fresh product. David Shepherd's policy is to "fund to production," meaning that he would advocate installing a freezer only if it was warranted by the size of the catch; he told me, regarding the Lolowai project, "I'll see them lose money and have fish go rotten before I'll put more money in." But Shepherd did help Silas obtain a loan for a freezer and arranged its installation in Lolowai.

The company's biggest problems centered on its young crew. Tom Daniels and Silas both worried that the crew were too young and inexperienced, but Silas had started the project with the explicit purpose of providing employment opportunities for boys in the Lovonda area, especially his teenage relatives. Crew members work for a percentage of gross sales rather than a fixed salary. Because the boys were young and knew little about fishing, they had limited success as fishermen. Because they caught so little fish, they earned very little money. They tended to become discouraged, losing all motivation to get up before dawn and go fishing. As Silas himself had found during his first job as a radio operator, Lolowai is a long way from Lovonda. Two hour's walking distance separates the two settlements, so the boys had to live at Lolowai while working for Jackers. After the initial excitement of the new boat wore off, Silas stayed in Lovonda and made the trip to Lolowai infrequently. He left his youngest brother, Eric, in charge of the crew.

In general, the young boys resented the fact that they earned nothing in the weeks when they were so unlucky as to catch nothing. They disliked Silas's reluctance to let them eat what they did catch; he told them that the Fisheries Department required the sale of the entire catch where possible. And they felt it was unfair for Eric to receive a much larger share than themselves.[10]

On average, a crew member on St. Peter's Star worked for only 2 consecutive months before returning to his home village. This pattern in itself does not indicate that the fishing project was unsuccessful. In fact, the opportunity to work intermittently at fishing fits well with existing patterns of copra production; it is consistent with a history of periodic labor migration in which young men travelled and worked on plantations before returning home and settling down;[11] and it allows many boys a chance to try their hand at fishing. The problem was that most boys quit after a few months aboard St. Peter's Star because they were unhappy. Eric, a teenager himself, was unable to provide the necessary leadership for the crew. While Silas recognized the problem and spoke of plans to have an older man live at Lolowai with the boys to make sure they went fishing regularly and to look after their food, he had done nothing to improve the situation by late 1985.

Traditionally, young men served as a source of labor for leaders, living in their men's houses, fighting their battles, and hunting their pigs. Today, leaders in Longana still tend to organize the labor of teenagers and unmarried men, whom they reward with food and with the generalized promise of support when the young men marry or kill pigs in the graded society. Silas modelled himself on these pre-eminent men when he let it be known that his fishing project was intended to benefit local youth by providing them with the chance to work for him. But he failed to provide the leadership necessary to make his imitation of traditional authority credible. Instead of admiring Silas's organizational ability, the parents of Longana crew members criticized Silas for his inadequate supervision of their sons. Not that the crew members got into trouble at Lolowai.[12] Rather, from the parents' point of view, their sons signed on with St. Peter's Star to gain work experience, eat fish, and earn money; it was Silas's lack of involvement in the day to day running of the project, they felt, that made it fail to live up to the young peoples' expectations.

By June 1984, Tom felt he had taught those involved in Jackers all that he could and that it was time for him to work more as a fisheries extension officer, finding fishing grounds and helping others in the area, than as an advisor to Jackers. The Fisheries Department provided Tom with a single-hulled boat. He began to help two projects in West Ambae, a project at the Catholic mission on the north coast, and groups at Vureas High School and Torgil, where a canoe big enough for deep sea fishing was outfitted with two handreels.

As Silas gradually realized that fishing was not going to be very profitable, especially if he remained peripheral to the daily running of the project, his interest turned to other entrepreneurial ventures. He revitalized his store in Lovonda, concentrating on sales of tinned fish; as he explained to me with a grin, fresh fish from the project seldom reached Lovonda and he was sorry to see his relatives and neighbors hungry for fish.

Another of Silas's business ideas was to start a kava bar at Lolowai where residents could gather to drink the popular and mildly narcotic infusion made from the roots of a kind of pepper plant. As at the beginning of his fishing project, Silas's rationale was one of helping the youth; "it would be good if we had something else going on the side, so if the boys weren't making much money fishing, there would still be some money that they could be earning. People in the Lolowai area are very eager to drink kava and I thought, well, the money from a kava bar wouldn't be wasted; we would put it right into the fishing project." Tom Daniels strongly opposed Silas's plans to open a kava bar, feeling that it would encourage kava drinking among the crew at some expense to the fishing effort. Silas resented Tom's opposition to what the Longanan had thought was a good idea.

Silas also resented Tom's attempts to treat Jackers as a community project. Although the company was composed of at least seven members who had purchased $25 shares, Tom came to realize that Jackers was a one man show. Tom's efforts to encourage shareholders meetings and to introduce a voting procedure for decision-making were not welcomed. Few meetings were held, and Silas continued to make all the decisions for the company.

Finally, Silas resented Tom's decreasing involvement in the Jackers project once the VFA had his own boat. Although the two men were not congenial, Silas felt that Tom should remain with the project that he had been sent to Lolowai to assist. Silas wanted Tom to sell any fish he caught to Jackers; then Jackers would sell the fish to the Lolowai people. But when Tom came ashore from a fishing trip, he sold his catch directly to Lolowai consumers. This made Silas angry; he no longer wanted anything to do with Tom.

The deteriorating relationship between the two men erupted in open hostility on July 9, 1984. It was a Monday. Silas was working on the Fisheries house—or as he called it "my house"—by the shore of Lolowai Bay. Rhythmically wielding a machete, he was a cutting a tree to use as a housepost when Tom arrived. The Canadian began a conversation with Silas about what to do with the cement that was left over from building the fisheries house. Suddenly, Silas burst into a rage. He brandished the machete and threatened to attack Tom with the knife. Silas doesn't remember exactly what it was that made him so angry: "I just remember saying, 'All the time you speak so harshly to me and now you are going to know who I really am!' " "The only thing that kept me from cutting him with my knife," Silas added, "was that I was thinking about prison, and I didn't want to go to prison for attacking him. The other thing was that I knew I was a leader in the village, and it wouldn't be good if I attacked a man."

It was impossible for Silas and Tom to work together after this episode. In late August, Tom left Lolowai with Mary and their daughter for a holiday. They travelled by outrigger canoe along the north coast of Ambae, camping, visiting villages along the way, and enjoying the chance to have a unique vacation. They returned to Lolowai where they remained until the end of Tom's contract in May 1985.

St. Peter's Star continued fishing following more or less the same pattern as when Tom had worked closely with the project (see Figure 5). The volume of business varied from month to month, but overall the trend was encouraging. From a low of $200 in October, monthly fish sales increased to $450 in November and a record high of $700 in December 1984.

Then in January 1985, Cyclone Nigel struck Vanuatu, devastating Ambae. The Lolowai area was especially hard hit; most of the buildings at Vureas High School were left roofless; a cargo ship was blown onto the rocks at Lolowai Bay. St. Peter's Star was damaged in the storm. Fortunately, Silas had paid an overdue bill for insurance on the boat just a few days before the cyclone struck. The company was unable to fish for the second half of January, all of February and part of March while repairs were made to the boat, first on Ambae and then at the Santo boatyard.

In April, Jackers' crew was able once again to fish regularly aboard St. Peter's Star. The monthly catch was the company's highest ever, with sales in excess of $750. In May, Tom Daniels left Lolowai at the end of his contract. Although Tom had had virtually nothing to do with the Jackers project for almost a year, his mere presence in the area and the interest he encouraged in fishing may have had a positive

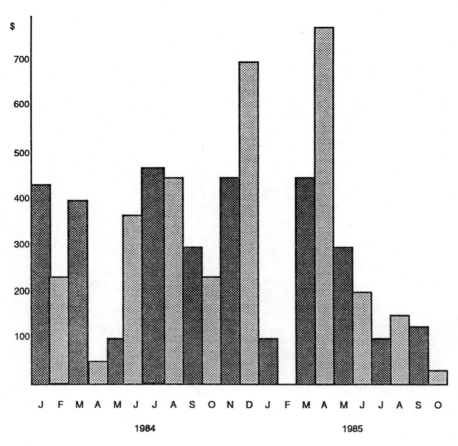

FIGURE 5
Jackers Fishing Company Monthly Sales

effect on Jackers' level of effort. Jackers' sales dropped to $300 in May, beginning a downward slide that had reached a low of $8 in sales for the month of October when I arrived to do the research for this book.

Silas did not miss a payment to the Development Bank in the first two years of the project. The cyclone's damage to his boat had delayed his March payment, but he managed to submit the money soon after St. Peter's Star was back in operation. In addition, Silas had to pay $400 per year for insurance on the boat and make "contributions" toward the cost of the freezer that had been supplied by Fisheries.[13] By 31 October 1985, Silas had reduced his Development Bank loan from $4000 to $1675.[14] The repayment of the loan constituted approximately 30 percent of Jackers' expenses, comparable to the cost of crews' wages and fuel.

When I left Ambae in December 1985, it seemed unlikely that Silas would soon make another loan payment. St. Peter's Star went on shorter and shorter trips, often no more than an hour in the morning with sometimes a second sortie at dusk. The catches ranged from poor to none at all. The two newest crew members, who had worked for two or three months, were ready to quit. Even Eric, the secretary/captain was becoming very discouraged. At the end of November, the boys all went home because the fuel for the boat was exhausted and there was not enough money in the cash box to buy another drum, even at duty-free prices. After 24 months of fishing, Jackers showed a credit balance of only $64 (see Table 1).

With a commitment to pay the captain and crew a total of 31 percent

TABLE 1
Jackers's Income and Expenses (December 1983–October 1985)

| Date | Income | | | Expenses | | | | | |
	Fish Sales	Other Income	Total	Fuel	Equip-ment	Misc.	Crews Pay	Loan	Total
12/83	538	27	565		15	44	126		185
1/84	420	53	473	87	70	53	110		320
2/84	238	13	252	189	45	7	74		315
3/84	401		401	178		29	105	389	312
4/84	52	19	71	177	65	84	150		476
5/84	103		103			20	14		34
6/84	377	1	378	125		125	108		358
7/84	484	14	498	63	10	35	157		265
8/84	466	29	495	63	35	52	129	389	668
9/84	307	2	309	122	38	39	114		313
10/84	231	22	253	59		51	84		194
11/84	445		445	122	7	49	131	389	698
12/84	701	47	748	62		44	173		279
1/85	93	2	95			395	31		426
2/85	no fishing because of hurricane damage								
3/85	453		453	130	15	18	133	389	685
4/85	758	26	784	131	3	163	235		532
5/85	306	52	358	142	14	72	90		318
6/85	192	8	200	94	10	41	36		181
7/85	98	1	99	90		14	32		136
8/85	150		150	90		35	53		178
9/85	133		133	90	5	35	21	389	41
10/85	8	57	65	74			17		91

of gross earnings, as well as loan obligations and expenses for fuel and gear, it is hardly surprising that the Longana project had cleared a grand total of only $64 in its first two years of operation. Given the project's operating costs and the frequency of fishing trips (an estimated 16 per month) the project would have had to sell at least 384 kg of fish per month to earn enough money just to cover expenses, much less make a profit.[15] In other words, the project was losing about $125 each month in 1985.

Before I left, I asked Silas if he was tired of fishing. "As for myself," he replied, "I'm not tired of it. But then I'm not the one who is going fishing. It's the young boys whom we have to keep interested. I don't really want to fish. I want to be the manager and organize them from the shore."

Expectations Fulfilled?

On almost every count, Jackers has so far failed to match the expectations of the Fisheries Department. While the company may yet succeed, in the sense of becoming an ongoing, viable small business, it is unlikely ever to operate on the scale that the department anticipated. The project document that the department filed with the Development Bank when Jackers started shows estimated earnings of $11,520 per year, with expenses totalling $9,574 and an annual profit of almost $2,000 (see Table 2). The project's actual earnings amounted to far less than this, only about $3,966 per annum over the first 24 months. The whole project operated on a smaller than expected scale. Expenses totalled only $3,934 annually, leaving a profit that amounted to small change by the standards of the project document.

Only in the number of fishing trips made each year did Jackers operate on the same scale as the department expected. The project document estimated that Silas's boat would make four fishing trips a week for 40 weeks of the year. In fact, the boat made as many as 180 trips a year. But these were short and not very productive excursions. Only 4 percent of the trips returned with more than 50 kg of fish. More than half of the trips returned with less than 10 kg of fish, and 18 percent of the time the boat returned with no catch at all.

These catches seem particularly poor when compared with the planners' estimates that the project would yield 50–60 kg per trip, sixteen times a month. Clearly, these estimates are unrealistic. But it is still hard to understand how a project that had benefited from the presence of a Canadian volunteer for two years could return from the sea, day after day, with such poor catches. The explanation lies partly in the inexperience of the crew, partly in the depletion of virgin

TABLE 2
Fisheries Project Document for Jackers Fishing Company

---

4 fishing trips/week, 40 weeks/year
160 trips/year
60 kg/trip: 9600 kg/year
Sold at $1.20/kg; $11,520 gross year

Expenses/year	
Depreciation of boat (6 years)	$1,070
Depreciation of 25 hp (3 years)	300
Depreciation of 8 hp (5 years)	120
Loan repayment	1,553
Fuel 20 L/trip at 63 VT/L	2,016
Oil and grease	200
Maintenance and repairs	350
Fish gear replacement	300
Bait	500
Wages (4 crew at 5% each + secretary, 4%)	2,765
Insurance	400
TOTAL	$9,574

Source: Fisheries Department of the Vanuatu government.

stocks of deep water snappers in the spots to which St. Peter's Star returned again and again, and partly in the requirement that the boat file a record of daily fishing effort in order to obtain duty-free fuel. The record of a quick trip out of Lolowai Bay at dawn, returning empty-handed an hour later would be enough to fulfill the letter of the Fisheries Department requirement, if not its spirit.

The crew's despondency is the simplest explanation for the extremely poor catches. The return to labor was so low from the project that there seemed no point in prolonging fishing trips. As a wage laborer, a man could earn $8 per day making copra.[16] In Port Olry, men who crewed on fishing boats earned about $6.50 per day, with the possibility of a big catch now and again in which crew members, working for a percentage of fish sales, could earn far more than they were certain to earn making copra. But in Longana this was not the case. The boys who crewed on St. Peter's Star earned an average of $20 per month in 1985, or $1 per working day. No wonder the turnover among the crew is so rapid and only teenagers are willing to participate in the project.

Nevertheless, the Fisheries Department could consider Jackers to be a potential success. The fishing boat and the freezer still work, Silas and a few others now know how to fish in deep water. The Lolowai community still wants to eat top quality fish. The possibility remains for Jackers to become a thriving small business. But so far that potential remains unfulfilled. $64 in the bank at the end of two years is a slim return considering that capital investment in the project (including the freezer) comes to almost $12,000, plus the cost of posting Tom Daniels to Lolowai and the cost to the government in foregone duty on fuel and fishing gear. It seems unlikely that Jackers will become the kind of "permanent" fishing project that the Fisheries Department seeks to establish, but it is too early to be sure.

For Tom Daniels, working as a CUSO cooperant in Lolowai was a learning experience that was positive in the long run. He took considerable satisfaction from his early work with Jackers and from the contribution he was able to make to helping other fishermen in the area. But he could not view Jackers as a success; not only was it in economic straits, it was run by a man who seemed opportunistic, who had acquired a boat simply because it was cheaper than a truck, and who lacked a commitment to fishing. A project such as Jackers could be of limited benefit to the community because it was not really a community project. Instead it was run by one man, a man who had considerable experience consuming development, and not by a group of islanders with a greater commitment to making the project a success in local terms.

Notes

1. My husband and I have described what happened when I became seriously ill with what we thought was a chlorquin-resistant strain of malaria. The Longanans suspected that spirits, not mosquitoes, had brought on my illness, and insisted on treating me appropriately with spells and leaf medicine (W & M Rodman, forthcoming). We have also dealt with sorcery, illness, and death in M & W Rodman 1983.

2. I follow Hammel and Laslett's (1974) definition of the household as the minimum domestic group who shares the same physical space (e.g., a house and a separate kitchen in the case of Longana). The concept of a residential segment refers to a more extensive domestic group. I have defined it as "the kin and affines outside the household with whom one is most closely involved in production and consumption activities and who occupy adjacent space" (Rodman 1985b:60).

3. A number of anthropologists working in the Pacific have characterized cash crop producers there as peasants (e.g., Finney 1973a, 1973b; Howlett 1973, Meggitt 1971). Two studies dealt directly with the characteristics attributed to peasants in Papua New Guinea (Amarshi, Good and Mortimer 1979; Fitzpatrick 1980), and these influenced my own interpretation of Longana in my dissertation (Rodman 1981). Subsequently (e.g., Rodman 1987a, 1987c), I have felt the term "peasant" simply has too many connotations from our own

cultural heritage; it is very difficult for a reader not to associate the term with feudalism, or dirndl skirts and clogs, or some other image of the peasant formed in our own childhood.

More seriously, the term "peasant" connotes a structural relationship in which the peasantry is exploited by a dominant class. To find this exploitation in Vanuatu requires a good deal of intellectual gymnastics. Further, it now seems to me that not only the term "peasant" but also the characteristics we attribute to the peasantry are somewhat our own creation. The attributes of the peasantry vary at least partly in accordance with the career of ideas in anthropology. I don't think the people who are intermittent producers of such commodities as copra **are** generally more independent than they were ten years ago, but today anthropologists **see** such people as having a much greater influence over the quality of their own lives than they were seen to have as "victims of progress" (Bodley 1975) only a few years ago. For a recent argument regarding the anthropological creation of the peasantry see the conclusion of Joel Kahn's review article (1985).

4. See Rodman (1983) for a description of how powerful leaders in the period of raiding prior to conversion and pacification in the 1930s acquired large amounts of land.

5. See Brookfield with Hart (1971).

6. See Roseberry (1985:25) who observes "there is no necessary connection between a strategy of household reproduction and an orientation toward use value."

7. There were some opportunities for rural entrepreneurs to diversify, notably in cocoa growing and cattle raising (see Rodman 1987c, Chapter 5). The only available abattoir, at Vureas High School on the other side of Lolowai from Longana, has operated intermittently and there has been little demand for Longana beef. Cattle graze under coconuts. They are killed and dressed in the plantation when someone needs meat for a feast. There is no butcher. Some cocoa is produced in Longana but black pod disease and the relatively stringent demands cocoa places on producers compared to copra have limited its popularity.

8. This is generally true of societies where reciprocity and kin-based social relations predominate. For examples of redistributive demands on Melanesian entrepreneurs see Finney (1973a) and Howlett (1973). See Gregory (1982) for evidence that the cash economy has served to re-energize the gift economy, which is based on exchanges between kin.

9. Note the similarity with the significance of a target amount—e.g., head tax, school fees, the price of a plane ticket—which has long motivated the production of copra in the islands (Rodman 1987c, chapter 5).

10. All told, 31 percent of Jackers' gross income has been distributed in wages, such that two crew members receive 7 percent each, a secretary/crew member earns 8 percent, and the captain receives 9 percent. (The Fisheries Department recommends that crews' wages in VFDP project total 25 percent of gross income. Silas was aware of this recommendation; 31 percent was a sign of his generosity with the crew and reflected the fact that an Alia catamaran requires four fishermen while a Hartley needs only two.) In 1985, Eric served as

both captain and secretary. Thus he paid himself 17 percent in contrast to the two remaining crew members' 7 percent. The absence of a fourth crew member meant that fishing was limited to three of the catamaran's four reels.

Only one other young man had worked with the project for as long as Eric; four others had served as crew members off and on for between six and ten months. Another 19 boys worked for periods ranging from less than one month to a maximum of five months.

11. See the special issue of Pacific Viewpoint on mobility, especially the article by Bonnemaison (1985) on rootedness and mobility in Vanuatu.

12. One crew member was killed in a drunken fight after a graded society ceremony in 1985, but this occurred in the boy's home village and had nothing to do with Silas or the fishing project.

13. Exactly what the arrangement was regarding payment for the freezer remained opaque to me. At one point it looked as if the International Human Assistance Program would supply the freezer. Tom objected to the idea of giving the freezer to Jackers cost-free, feeling that the fishing project had to pay something in order to avoid a "cargo mentality." According to David Shepherd, Silas was sending "$40 or $50 every now and then" to pay for the freezer. Jackers records show that $100 had been paid toward the freezer by October 1985, but other payments may have been made under the heading "Misc."

14. Because the cost of an Alia catamaran was about half-again as much as the Hartley fishing boat, the Fisheries Department was considering reducing the loan burden of projects with catamarans by as much as $1000.

15. If, however, the project had caught the 54 kg per trip that planners had anticipated, only 5 trips would have been necessary each month to catch 270 kg and yield a 7 percent profit. The project's actual 1985 catch was about 15 kg per trip, with about 15 trips made per month.

Fish prices in the projects I studied ranged between 95 cents and $1.20 per kg. I have used an average price of $1.07/kg in calculations for this and the following chapter. The figure of 270 kg/month is based on a monthly loan and insurance burden (paid quarterly) of $130 and crews' wages of 31 percent of gross earnings. Planners' estimates of catch per 4 hr trip vary from 50 to 60 kg. If the project caught 54 kg per trip, 5 trips would be required to catch 270 kg.

Estimated operating expenses for each trip are about $10, based on $1 for gear, a minimum of $7 for fuel (at 35 cents/liter duty free calculated at 5 liters/hr for a 4 hr trip); I have added $2 per trip in Longana because the Alia catamaran used in the project consumed more fuel than the smaller boats on which fuel consumption trials were conducted. The operating cost per trip in Port Olry was also about $10 per trip; while fuel consumption in the smaller Port Olry boats came to only about $7 per trip, fishermen there had to purchase ice (because they were selling to an urban market and high quality fish preservation was crucial) which cost about $2 per trip. All in all, the estimated operating costs seem valid for Port Olry where considerable fisheries research has taken place. But operating costs in the Longana project ran about 100 percent higher than the estimate in 1985. Expenditures on fuel and gear were twice what they should have been for the size of the catch.

This was so because the estimated catch of 54 kg is unrealistic. Fishermen went out much more often than five times a month. In fact, the Longana project fished at least four trips a week, as the Fisheries Department had assumed it would in writing the project document for Longana. But instead of catching 54 kg per trip, 16 times a month, 55 percent of all fishing trips that the Longana project undertook in 1985 caught less than 10 kg of fish for sale.

If 16 trips were required to catch 270 kg, the average catch per trip would come to 17 kg, a much more realistic figure. But the resulting $18 in sales per trip would leave the project with a deficit per trip of $5.65, given the cost of fuel, loan repayment, and crews wages.

To break even, the Longana project would have to have earned $26 from 24 kg of fish per trip, and made 16 fishing trips per month. But in fact, the project earned only an average of $15 per trip and fished 15 times a month in the first 9.5 months of 1985.

16. Rural wages in 1985 were about $2 per green (unprocessed) bag of copra.

8

A TROUBLED COMMUNITY

Expatriates have been attracted to Port Olry since at least 1887 when the Catholic mission first acquired land there. It is easy to understand why this is so, without taking into account the many practical reasons, such as fresh water, relative accessibility, and a healthy climate in comparison with other parts of Espiritu Santo Island. Port Olry is a picture postcard place; it is irresistible to us westerners whose culture created the fantasy of the South Seas paradise.

But Port Olry is also a troubled community that has yet to transcend the artificial basis for its existence. A Catholic mission drew people to this beautiful location, but neither the mission nor local residents seem able to forge groups with different origins and languages into a single community or to create a widespread sense of social responsibility. Let me try to convey first the beauty and then the problems; both characterize the quality of life in Port Olry.

My fieldnotes record that I spent the afternoon of 17 October 1985 sitting on the beach at Port Olry with two fishermen. We sat in the shade of a *na tavoa* tree. Over our heads, tiny white butterflies darted among the leaves like Christmas tree decorations come to life. The sandy pathways of the village at our backs were quiet in the early afternoon; the 600 residents were absent or, for the moment, muted. The children were in school and their chanting recitation was just out of earshot from where we sat. The adults had gone about their work in the gardens, in the copra plantations, or perhaps in town an hour's drive away. I sat with the fishermen on the beach while Radio Vanuatu played Vivaldi's Four Seasons, a rare interlude in the usual program of reggae, rock, and messages in the public interest about caring for one's teeth and registering the birth of one's children.

Sun had alternated with showers throughout the day. As we listened to Vivaldi and looked out to sea, a rainbow framed three canoes fishing on the horizon. The rainbow seemed to rise from the island of Malai to our left, or north. Malai, I suppose, is really an islet for we could wade there from the village at low tide and then wade farther, crossing to the larger Dolphin Island where sharp, jungle-clad cliffs rise from the sea and there is a fresh water lake in which to swim.

The rainbow arched across the sheltered bay. The tide was high and I could barely see where the ocean swell lifted to cross the reef; at low tide the waves broke, a flag of white waving now and again on the horizon. Inside the reef the water is so clear and the sand beneath the sea so white that the villagers say sharks, finding no hiding place, are frightened away by their own shadows. When I paddled a canoe with my son Sean in Port Olry, I had to laugh at my own vertigo. Floating on water so clear was, Sean said, what space flight must be like; we looked down on worlds amidst real grains of sand.

At the other end of the rainbow, to our right, the smallest islet, Malmat, added balance and symmetry to the view. In legend, the fishermen say, both Malai and Malmat are floating islands that travelled to Port Olry from somewhere else. In the same way, Araki, off whose coast I trolled around the fish aggregating device in Chapter 5, once was near Port Olry. But Araki suddenly floated away one day taking some men's wives and other women's husbands to its current location in South Santo, despite angry protestations from those left behind in Port Olry who thrashed the sea with sticks as the island sailed away.

A few hundred meters of open water separates Malmat from the main island. From the point where one comes ashore, a beach of the whitest sand curves for a kilometer or so back to the village, its sweep broken only by an occasional palm bent low over the beach and by the wreckage of the fighter plane that crashed there in World War II. It is a perfect beach—perfect for children learning to swim, perfect for a teenage boy to gallop a horse, perfect for a fisherman to cast his net. It is the ultimate window over the kitchen sink for the Port Olry women who scour their pots with sand. It is too perfect to leave alone, in the view of many outsiders who imagine replacing the villagers' cement and corrugated iron houses with picturesque bungalows, placing the restaurant just here and the tennis courts just there. So far, these imaginings are purely fantasy. But even to an anthropologist or a volunteer committed to the notion that "small is beautiful" Port Olry's physical charms are hard to resist. Ken Ford, the CUSO Village Fisheries Advisor posted to Port Olry in 1983, did not try to resist. Neither did I.

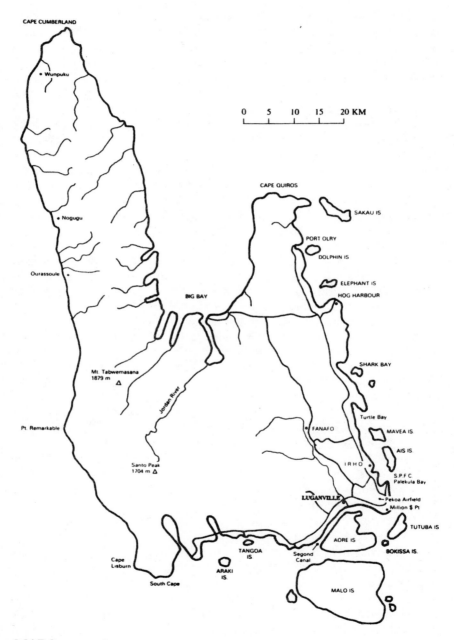

MAP 3
Santo Island

I sat on the beach with the two fishermen, listening to Vivaldi, watching the three canoes cross the distant reef, and contemplating the rainbow. One of the fishermen spoke, "You know Ken Ford didn't know where he was going to be sent in Vanuatu." The fisherman turned and pointed to the hill behind us toward the south where the road from town turns down into the village. He continued, "The Fisheries Department drove Ken out here in a truck. When they came around the corner of that hill up there, Ken saw this place. He looked down at Port Olry and he said, 'Ah, This is it! If they try to send me anywhere else I'm going home to Canada.' The department did try to send him to Ambae and to Tanna, but he wouldn't consider going."

On September 31st, we had our first visitors in Port Olry. I had been in the village for two days, living with my family in the bamboo house that Ken Ford and his wife had vacated the previous year. David Shepherd, manager of the Village Fisheries Development Program, drove into the village followed by a second 4-door, yellow Fisheries truck. A Japanese woman and three men climbed down from the trucks. They presented a cosmopolitan appearance, the men in chic safari-style khaki shirts and trousers, the woman in a silky dress and a head scarf. These visitors were in the midst of a one week trip to Vanuatu to discuss the possibility of giving $1–2 million in aid to fisheries development in the archipelago. David said he was bringing them on the "usual tourist route" up through Champagne Beach to take a look at the fishing association in Port Olry, then back to the comforts of the Hotel Santo in Luganville by nightfall.

I walked with David and the Japanese from our house, located next to the road, through the mission's coconut palm plantation to Remre Fishing Association about 400 m distant at the edge of the beach. Both the house we were occupying and the fishing association are bamboo structures with concrete floors set within sight of each other on the southern fringe of the village. There are no other houses nearby. Most of the village of some 600 people is concentrated in a clear sandy area toward the northern end of the beach, with a scattering of houses inland among the coconut palms.

David introduced the Japanese visitors to Manuel Cevouar, the young chief of Port Olry and manager of the fishing association. On that day Manuel wore a large straw hat and was smooth shaven—he grew a beard, then shaved it off during the five weeks I lived in the village. A dark, bright-eyed man in his twenties, Manuel knew how to deal with visitors. He would be polite to the Japanese, for he knew they were a potential source of "cargo" and he wanted an icemaker for Remre Association. At other times he could be antagonistic and hostile. As he explained to me, he tolerates white officials' frequent visits for only one reason: it is obvious to Manuel that a great deal of aid money is coming into Vanuatu and he wants his share.

Manuel and David showed the Japanese the facilities in the fishing association, which cost about $11,000 to establish. A central bay for receiving, weighing and cleaning fish separates the manager's office, on the left, from the walk-in coolroom on the right. A Kirby chill unit installed in the coolroom requires about three hours to bring fish down to a temperature of -5° C. The unit is powered by a 3 cylinder Lister diesel generator housed in an earth-banked shelter outside the fishing association building.

While the Japanese were inspecting the building, one of the local fishing boats came in to sell its catch. David Shepherd was amused by this good luck. He whispered to me that some people had been known to stage this sort of show, taking fish out of a coolroom, tossing it into an ice chest on a small boat, then sending the boat's crew out "fishing" with instructions to come ashore just as the aid donors arrive. Today, there was no need for artifice. A Port Olry man named Pierre had brought his 5 m boat in with three 5 kg *mahimahi*, two sea perch weighing a couple of kg each, and a fine looking 1 kg *pristipomoides* or "poulet" which I bought for our supper. In addition, Pierre had caught about 10 kg of smaller mixed snappers. David Shepherd said these fish were only "babies" and suggested that Pierre use a larger sized hook to ensure that he caught only mature snappers.

David then led the Japanese down the beach, walking from the fishing association toward the central part of the village. Along the way, they admired the 14 motorboats and 20 canoes that were pulled up on the beach at the time. Two of the Japanese men produced tape measures and busily noted the dimensions of the fishing boats. David Shepherd drew their attention to a handmade dinghy fitted with two hand reels and a small Suzuki outboard motor, an example, David observed, of local ingenuity and enthusiasm for fisheries development. He did not seem to realize (and I did not know at the time) that the boat's builder was a man who opposed the Fisheries Department's project; he undercut Remre by purchasing fish locally and selling to private buyers in town.

"What does the name of the fishing association, Remre, mean?" asked the Japanese woman, holding her shoes as she walked in the powdery sand. David replied that Remre means, roughly, "try again." This was Port Olry's third attempt to establish a fishing association; the previous associations had ended in financial disarray and had intensified antagonisms between factions in the village. "Why, then, has the Fisheries Department supported Remre in view of these earlier failures?" the woman asked. There were three reasons, in

Shepherd's opinion. First, a CUSO volunteer (Ken Ford) had been available to spend two years training a Port Olry manager; in this way, the "management problems" that had plagued the earlier associations might be avoided. Second, a market for local fish could now be guaranteed, which had not been possible in the past. But, according to David, the most important reason for Fisheries' support of the project was that the *whole village was involved in Remre.* Such total involvement, Shepherd felt, led to frequent disputes regarding the association; but he was also convinced, he told the potential aid donor, that only with the participation of the whole village could Remre succeed.

The whole village does participate in Remre, I found, but not in ways that encourage the association's success. Most fishermen, in fact, are not members of the fishing association; most of Remre's shareholders are not fishermen. The large number of fishing boats on the beach that day signified the fishermen's dissatisfaction with Remre. With a few exceptions such as Pierre, they were "on strike" until conditions improved. The weather was no good for fishing they said; but the wind was fair.[1] What they meant was that they found the social and economic climate intolerable for commercial fishing.

Port Olry's picture-perfect appearance distracts the eye. But a look beyond the sea, the beach, and the palms to the people suggests that this is a troubled community. One look at the local meeting house reveals that, although new, the building is neglected. Cattle have breached the barbed wire fence and poke their heads through broken louvered windows. There are no flowers around the meeting house, a sign, people say, of the current crisis of leadership in the village. For another sign one need only look at the villagers after mass on Sunday. They stream out of the massive white church built on a rise at the north end of the settlement. Without a pause for conversation, everyone walks quickly toward his or her home. Even children do not linger. There is no place for casual camaraderie when the whole village comes together. Even walking to and from the gardens on week days, most people do not speak when they pass each other on a path.

One day, Pascaline, the Port Olry woman who worked with me on the study, and I were walking near the shore. She spotted a little boy, five or six years old, standing alone on the beach sniffling and chucking stones into the sea. Pascaline, 20 years old and not yet married, had worked previously as housemistress to children boarding at the mission school. She had a keen interest in children, and in the school she spoke to them in any one of a variety of languages—French, Bislama, Tolomako and, her first language, Sakao. She first spoke to the boy in

Bislama; "Where did you sleep last night?" The little boy was silent; he kept looking out across the water. Pascaline addressed him in Tolomako, which she said was his native language, but the child still ignored her. Finally, she left him to his silence and, as we walked away, explained to me that the child's mother and father "don't like him." Sometimes his grandmother lets him sleep in her house, but sometimes he just sleeps in the bush.

Finally, one has only to look, as I did one evening at sunset, at the villagers' response when a fishing boat comes ashore in order to see that Port Olry is different from most Vanuatu communities. Most afternoons I spent the hour or so before sunset on the beach with my children and Pascaline. One evening we watched as two fishermen returned after four days spent deep water fishing and four nights spent sleeping in a cave on shore far from the village. My journal records what I saw:

> 11 October 1985   Port Olry
> I was amazed that when B. and P. returned about 5:30 [p.m.] from four days' fishing in Big Bay not one person went out to greet them. They came ashore very quickly, having sped through the lagoon and hit the beach like a landing craft. Perhaps eight men were sitting on the beach off the village when the boat came ashore just below the wrecked airplane. Nobody went to greet them although the men all watched the arrival with interest. The two fishermen, visibly exhausted, struggled to haul the boat up on the beach by themselves. Not even the kids ran down the beach to check things out. Port Olry is not your average Melanesian village.

Port Olry is a town, but in many ways it is not a community.

When I asked local residents about the quality of life in Port Olry, most commented that physically the living was easy. There are ample opportunities for earning money in the village. In addition to commercial fishing, these opportunities include copra and cocoa production, 10 stores, 16 truck-taxi businesses, gardening for the twice weekly trip to the Luganville produce market,[2] collection of coconut crabs, sales of pigs to the South Pacific Fishing Company at Palekula, sales of cattle to SASI (the Santo abattoir), and sales of lobster to the fishing association and to Chinese buyers in Luganville. There is easy access to bountiful supplies of fish, shellfish, wild birds, fruit, and vegetables. The Boucheries de Brousse ("bush butcher") provides Port Olry with top quality local beef. Two firms in Luganville send minibuses full of warm French bread speeding into the village before dawn three times a week.

But in social terms, villagers feel that their quality of life has deteriorated over the years. In part, they see this deterioration as the only negative consequence of the extension of the road from Luganville to Port Olry in the 1960s. The road allowed the village to achieve prosperity in financial terms, but it also led people to seek solutions to their problems in town rather than within the village. Most legal disputes are processed in Luganville. The town is an easy source of alcoholic beverages. In some ways the town that used to be too far away is now too near.

Older residents seem most aware of the deterioration in community life. Some blatantly romanticize the past. One graybeard's eyes misted over as he told me, "In the old days, men used to be really men. They were taller and fatter than we are now because they ate cooked food only once a day, in the evening. The rest of the day they lived off the land. They were strong people who could break thick branches with their bare hands and spear big fish."

Others offer more realistic criticisms. I met with Guillaume and his wife in their house inside a compound fenced against the mission cattle with barbed wire and frangipani. Their house had grown to accommodate seven children, three of whom were now married. We met in a large room about 8 m by 5 m, from which several bedrooms and an open air kitchen radiated. Each wall of the structure seemed to be made of a different material—corrugated iron, fibrolite, bamboo, cement block. Large, multicolored paper globes fashioned from unthinkable numbers of chewing gum wrappers hung decoratively from the ceiling. Guillaume, a portly man with an easy smile, clearly led a comfortable life. But he wasn't happy with Port Olry. "The place is good," he said. "The people are the problem. Some people here might try to save your life, but others . . ." He shrugged, "No, many won't even stop a truck to give you a lift. No one has any respect for anyone else. Too much beer. Parties are disastrous. People will beat you up in your own house." If this is so, I asked, why are alcohol-related deaths or serious injuries uncommon? Guillaume replied that the only reason there aren't more deaths or injuries is that people drink together in large groups so it is relatively easy to break up fights. "Alcohol has been around a long time, but never in this quantity," he added, "It was better in the old days—then we had only gin and cognac!" In Guillaume's view, Port Olry has changed, and not for the better. When he was a young man, the village was a quiet place. Swearing was the only frequent legal offence. But nowadays, in Guillaume's opinion, little kids swear in ways for which an adult would have been fined a tusked pig in the past. "We can see that we are in the midst of change," Guillaume concluded. "We are not like our fathers and not like our sons."

Not Like Our Fathers, Not Like Our Sons

Port Olry's social composition is as artificial as its beauty is natural. It is a western creation, and the lack of a sense of social responsibility in Port Olry today reflects the history of the village.

Two Catholic priests, Père Pionnier and Père Deniau, obtained land for a mission at Port Olry in October 1887, the year that French priests and New Caledonian catechists established a permanent Catholic presence in several locations in Vanuatu after limited earlier efforts at conversion in the archipelago.[3] The first congregations were made up of immigrants from the island of Sakao to the north and other Sakao language speakers who believed their ancestors had always lived in Port Olry, which they called "Rotes" after a salt spring near what is now the fishing association, or "Latamav" after the curving beach. The site of the first mission was at the north end of the beach where a broad, tidal river, whose spring-fed source is only about a kilometer inland, meets the sea and provides a good boat landing.

The site of the mission was favorable in many ways, but it was not very safe. The community of about 20 local people was vulnerable to attack from warriors who came down from the hills. In 1918, two women from a hamlet in the Santo interior fled to the mission at Port Olry seeking sanctuary. Warriors pursuing the women found the Catholic priest, Père Pousi, on the veranda of his house, which was built on stilts to capture the sea breeze and the magnificent view. The warriors ripped the priest's clothing and tore it from his body; but they fled without doing further harm at the sound of an approaching ship. Although the boat was some distance from the shore its engine was very loud. Père Pousi hid until the boat arrived, then ran down to the river and climbed safely aboard the ship.

This episode precipitated the relocation of the community to Dolphin Island, just past Malai. Dolphin Island has very little arable land at the base of the island's cliffs, but there was room enough for a village, and the island provided some protection against unexpected visits from warriors of the sort who surprised Père Pousi. Gardens were still made ashore near the old mission site, but the threat of attack by warriors from the interior remained, and everyone returned to the small island at nightfall.

Meanwhile, another Catholic mission was operating at Tolomako in the Big Bay region of Santo not far from where Quiros, the first white man in Vanuatu, had landed in 1606. Unlike Port Olry, the mission at Tolomako was difficult to reach by sea, and malaria was a serious problem there because of the marshy terrain. The Catholic church concluded that it would be preferable to bring schoolchildren to Port Olry, so in 1920 the Tolomako mission was relocated. Manuel, the chief of the Tolomako people, whose grandson and namesake is the current chief of Port Olry, led his followers to join the converts already living on Dolphin Island.

The immigrants from Tolomako made gardens near what is now the southern end of Port Olry village, while the original residents gardened at the north end of the settlement. At first, missionaries, Tolomako people, and those who had come from the Sakao Island–Port Olry area all lived together on Dolphin Island. Then, confident that the community was now large enough to deter raiders, they moved back to renovate the buildings in the settlement they had abandoned at the north end of the beach.

The Tolomako people, although matrilineal like the Sakao-speakers, have retained their own language, and in the early days there was no intermarriage between the two groups. Chief Manuel's brother wanted to marry a local woman soon after the Tolomako group arrived, but that, in the words of an old Port Olry man, "would have turned Dolphin Island upside down." Much later, the old chief himself married a Sakao woman after his first wife died; since then the groups have become intertwined but not blended, and relations between them can still be tense.

When the missionized community moved back to Port Olry from Dolphin Island, most of the current site of the village was covered with the dense jungle of secondary forest that takes over fallow gardens. The settlement has expanded a great deal since then. Today, the mission facilities consist of the church, a dispensary run by two French nuns, and a primary school with a staff of 13 including a ni-Vanuatu headmaster from another island. Schooling is in French. Some families live in Port Olry explicitly to allow their children access to the school there, maintaining second homes in villages in the interior of Santo.[4] Others send their children to school by canoe. At the river landing, I used to watch a scene that must have changed little since the 1920s. Every weekday morning, a bearded old man wearing only a red loincloth and a broad, black belt paddled his large canoe into the river from the direction of Cape Quiros. His cargo of six small schoolboys in clean shorts and t-shirts sat quietly in the bottom of the canoe; they burst into life as the canoe nosed up against the bank and ran off to their classrooms, lunch boxes clattering.

The mission community is still under the leadership of an expatriate priest, an Englishman who is fluent in French, speaks Bislama like a ni-Vanuatu, and spent 27 years on the island of Tanna in the south of Vanuatu before coming to Port Olry after the Santo Rebellion in 1980. He has a passion for butterflies—on Tanna, he discovered a new species which has been named after him—and an abiding commitment to the church in Vanuatu which has been his life's work. The mission employs four full-time workers and a stockman; teams of young men serve as "legionnaires" providing labor to turn the mission's 250 ha. of coconuts into copra at the rate of $2 per green or unprocessed bag.[5]

The priest recognizes that in terms of community spirit, the local quality of life is less than positive. There is a great deal of mistrust, he says, that has grown worse in recent years but that has deep historical roots. He seemed to speak metaphorically as well as literally when he commented to me that people will keep their own yards clean but it is hard to persuade them to clean up the village as a whole unless the mission provides a tractor.

The village begins along the beach just south of the mission. Several broad sandy paths that are unnamed streets run parallel to the beach. A great variety of house types hints at the villagers' deep-seated individuality. (See Figure 6.) Almost three-quarters of the houses are made of cement and other nontraditional materials.[6] All the houses within the mission boundary are built with the permission of the church, and residents are expected to comply with mission rules. In particular, there is a prohibition on the sale of alcohol, although residents bring in liquor for personal consumption from Luganville and a bar is located just outside the mission fence. Only the church's cattle can graze freely among the coconut plantation in which the village is set. Other animals must be tied or fenced. Animals astray are fair game for the priest; I have seen him swerve his truck off the road to round up a vagrant pig.

In October 1985, about 600 people lived in Port Olry and the central core of the village consisted of 427 people divided among 95 households. This central core constituted the research population for my study. 86 percent of these households were headed by a man, while single females headed the remaining 14 percent.[7]

Nominally, all of these households were under the leadership of an elected chief, who also happened to be the manager of the fishing association. Traditionally, leaders came gradually into positions of influence. As in Longana, rank-taking in a graded society was a source of prestige. In Santo, pig-killing earned a man the title of Moli which has come to be synonymous with "chief." But in both Longana and Santo, rank-taking alone was never enough to secure a position of leadership. One's "fasin," the Bislama term that connotes character and behavior, was what really mattered; and "fasin" is still the key to effective leadership today. A leader has to demonstrate his fairmindedness by appearing to treat his kinsmen no differently than he treats other neighbors. He has to be someone who doesn't lose his temper, who is good at resolving disputes. He has to know how to

FIGURE 6
Examples of House Types in Port Olry

reprimand without damaging peoples' self-esteem. Above all, the leader's own "fasin" has to be seen to be good; he has to practice what he preaches.

The Catholic mission brought an end to pig-killing. Local people, forbidden even to watch the traditional ceremonies, have lost most of the knowledge of how these rites were performed. The customary leader of Port Olry at the time of conversion was allowed to remain in charge of the village for his lifetime; but upon his death, the church took charge of the selection of new leaders. Instead of relying on men with the title "Moli," the missionaries chose new chiefs from among the faithful. Until the most recent chief, young Manuel, came to office, there have always been two appointed chiefs in the village, one representing the Big Bay people and one chosen from descendants of the original Sakao residents. In 1984, Manuel became the first chief to be chosen by an election.

The democratic process has altered political equations throughout Vanuatu and given new power to the country's youth.[8] In Port Olry, young voters succeeded in electing the candidate of their choice; the new chief, elected by a margin of only a few votes was Manuel Cevouar, the son of the previous chief and grandson of the first Manuel who had brought the immigrants from Tolomako to Port Olry. He won the support of young electors by promising new sports facilities and a nightclub. While sports have become important in the village—there are six football teams, a volleyball team, and a boxing club—the priest flatly vetoed the idea of a nightclub within the mission's territory.

By the time I arrived in Port Olry, Manuel clearly lacked the support of most of the village. He was not sought out to resolve disputes within the community. He could not expect people even to come to a meeting if he were to call one. It seemed to the chief as if he was virtually alone in trying to accomplish things, such as organizing sporting events, that should have been community projects. None of the village committees were working smoothly. Everywhere in Port Olry, people had different ideas about what course the community should be following. The chief was not enforcing local laws, and he seemed especially to turn a blind eye to offences involving his immediate family. Obviously there was a crisis of leadership in the village with fairly deep historical roots. What was less obvious was that Manuel's position as manager of Remre Fishing Association was important to him because it provided him with a power base in the community.

The first stop for a Fisheries Department truck from Luganville arriving in Port Olry was Manuel's sister's kitchen. Celia could be counted on to offer cold lemonade, a few lighthearted jokes, and serious admonitions that so-and-so must be forbidden to buy fish in competition with Remre, or that local criticisms of Manuel were unfounded because they only reflected people's petty jealousies of the young leader's success. Later, if Manuel had organized a meeting, the Fisheries officer would speak to those assembled at the fishing association. Often he chastised the local people for failure to support "their" organization, admonishing the Port Olry residents that they started Remre, that the association belongs to them, and that they must support it. In the face of persistent local opposition to Manuel, the Fisheries Department's response was to give him support as the person best qualified for the job.

A Woman's Work

Women in Port Olry don't use canoes and don't often accompany their husbands on fishing trips. They almost never speak in public, and they are rarely seen to be entrepreneurs in their own right. But a woman, Celia Sarsom, is the prime mover behind Remre Fishing Association. The case that follows highlights several points: First, it shows how Melanesian women, like men, keep their options open and pursue strategies of self-reliance through diversification of productive activities. Second, the participation of one woman in a development project may actually jeopardize the interests of other women, in this case other villagers who sold fresh fish at the regional market before the refrigerated fishing project made such sales illegal. Third, by observing the patterns of this woman's daily routine rather than simply presenting people's verbal reconstruction of events associated with a fishing project the case illustrates the dynamics of a woman's participation in development. Although Celia never fished she played a crucial role in starting a major village fishing project.

Celia Sarsom has deep brown eyes that match her skin tone, and a laugh that roars through her small, fat body. In 1985, Celia was 44 years old and she was probably the most influential person in Port Olry although she held no office. Celia's style was to be tough, direct, and outspoken. But in public, she conformed to local expectations of feminine behavior. She dressed like the other women in clean, bright colored but unexceptional Mother Hubbards.[9] She sat with the other women on the fringes of social gatherings and on the left side of the church.

With her tall, soft-spoken husband, Philip, usually willing to follow her lead, she oversees the running of the family business. There are two trucks, a generator for household electricity, and a fishing boat to be kept running. The family store is the largest in Port Olry. The family lives above the store in the only two-storey structure in the village. Celia organizes the household's labor every evening at supper time. She presides over the table in the small structure that used to house the family but now serves as the kitchen. One of her daughters, Philippa, cooks while Celia evaluates the events of the day and plans for tomorrow.

I stayed with Celia for a few days in September 1985 before I began the Port Olry study. I sat with her at the kitchen table and watched her interact with her 3 sons, her 4 daughters, a baby, and her husband. The family gathered in the kitchen but there was no evening meal at which everyone sat down and ate together. People came and went, dipping into Philippa's cooking pots to heap their plates with rice and help themselves to a bit of fresh *mangru*, the fish that is a local favorite and is readily available close to shore. Celia talked to the baby, hugged her, spanked her fondly and was full of noisy affection for her. In a similar although less physical way she paid attention to each child. With many of the children she discussed sports. Clearly, she was an expert on the relative merits of soccer teams in the whole of Vanuatu.

At about 7 p.m., Philip returned from the copra dryer and fixed two plates of rice and fish. He gave the smaller one to Celia and sat down across the table from her, but before he could begin to eat she switched plates with him, taking the larger portion for herself with a playful scowl.

Celia had been awake since 3:30 a.m. when she left to sell vegetables from her garden at the Luganville market; but she sat at the table until the last son appeared at 9 p.m. She organized everyone's activities for the next day. The boys were to get firewood to smoke the copra. The girls were to feed the pigs and sew clothes for the baby. As for Philip, he was to transport a load of copra to town. To my embarrassment, she criticized Philip in Bislama for my benefit. He was foolish, in her opinion, because he had arranged to take someone's copra to Luganville next Wednesday but everyone knew, except Philip who hadn't been paying attention, she said, that the price of copra was due to drop next Tuesday, so he should take the copra to town tomorrow.

Celia's father, Marcel, was still the village chief when she first considered the idea of starting a new fishing association in Port Olry. It seemed a risky undertaking, partly because her father's reputation had foundered on an earlier community venture, the St. Boniface; subsequently, the leader of a rival faction in the village had attempted to establish a fishing association, but participants felt that the organizer was absconding with their money and the enterprise failed. Still the possibility of building up a viable fishing business intrigued Celia.

She thinks it was in 1980 that she and Philip began buying fish that local fishermen caught from their canoes using coiled handlines tied end to end to reach the depths where they knew the snappers lived. Celia held the fish in a kerosene freezer in her store. Twice a week she took the chilled fish, as well as any fresh fish she could arrange to purchase, to sell at the Luganville market. Soon she there were times when she had more fish than she could chill; the fish marketing business was bigger than she had expected.

One day in February 1982, Celia was approached at the market by a white man, a CUSO volunteer who had moved to Santo to organize village fisheries development in the north of Vanuatu. The Canadian had visited Port Olry to conduct a training course, and he recognized its potential. Soon after he introduced shark-proof line and new techniques for tying hooks, the Port Olry fishermen caught one tonne of fish in a single day from their canoes. Much of the catch spoiled on the beach. The Canadian knew that there was a large offshore fishing bank of the depth appropriate for deep water handlining; ice was available from the South Pacific Fishing Company at Palekula; there was easy access to Luganville and to the airport near town; and the volunteer had been impressed at the enthusiasm he found in Port Olry for fishing. Unlike islanders in many parts of Vanuatu, the Port Olry people were clearly oriented toward going out on the sea in small craft.

Gradually, the Canadian and Celia began to make plans. They talked repeatedly about how to start a viable fish marketing association in Port Olry. The Canadian was careful to be sure that Celia felt the people of Port Olry really wanted to start such an association. And he was careful to point out what the association might cost her personally. Three years later I spoke with the volunteer in his home in Canada. He recollected telling Celia that a new fishing association would drive her out of business. She would no longer be able to sell fresh or frozen fish at the market because, first, the association would handle all the fish from Port Olry and, second, the Fisheries Department would build a fish market with proper cold storage in Luganville and market women would no longer be allowed to sell fresh fish, both for health reasons and to reduce competition with the new market. He remembers Celia's response well because it surprised him; "That's great!" she said,"I don't need that work. I have more fish than I can handle, and I have more than enough other business." She seemed quite happy to put herself out of a job, but in a way she was only putting the other women who sold fish at the market out of work, for she immediately invested her own money and time in organizing Remre Fishing Association. Just as the Canadian volunteer saw potential in Port Olry fishermen, Celia quickly recognized the potential benefit to her family in organizing Remre as a village fisheries development project; she knew she would have the government and the expertise of Canadian fishermen on her side.

Celia's prominence in the community made it easy for CUSO and for representatives of the Vanuatu government to come to her when local input into decision-making was needed, rather than moving more deeply or more widely into the community. But it meant that the realistic assessment of programming options was limited to the view of one faction (Celia's) in this instance. By the mid-1980s, Celia's political faction was a tiny minority in the village, although it was still able to dominate the fishing association because Celia still had the support of the Fisheries Department and CUSO. Celia's faction also continued to be far more influential in village politics than the number of its supporters would indicate, a measure of the extent to which the support of institutions external to the village, such as Fisheries and CUSO, can contribute to local political capital.

As this chapter has shown, the relationship of Celia's powerful but small faction to the rest of the community can only be understood in an historical perspective. Fisheries development has intensified this factionalism by siding with Celia's group. Although the fishing association was introduced as a "community" development project, it was incorporated into the village from the beginning as if it were an offshoot of Celia's family business. Prospects for the venture's success as a community venture were bleak in any case. First, a community project is best suited to a village with a strong sense of community. For historical reasons, Port Olry has never been such a place. Second, the fishing association should be under the control of the community if it were really a community project; instead, the Fisheries Department's efforts to support the association have at times over-ruled community decisions and otherwise interfered with the will of the community.

For CUSO personnel in Vanuatu, Celia posed a problem to which there was no easy solution. Here was a woman, a strong Melanesian woman with clear ideas about development and the perseverance to accomplish her goals. With the Canadian International Development Agency's emphasis on including a women's component in development projects, Celia seems in many ways the ideal focus for a fishing project. Yet the CUSO staff knew that she also manipulated them, and that by dealing with the village through her and her relatives they were unable to communicate with the many local fishermen who mistrusted Celia's faction.

Here is an indication of how CUSO attempted to deal with this issue. Celia had encouraged CUSO to let me stay in her house while I conducted an evaluation of the Remre project in 1985. She could charge

CUSO for room and board, but more importantly, she could also oversee my research. I spent three days with her preliminary to the study; she guided me from one of her advocates to the next, full of energy and good-will. By this time, CUSO had already recognized the wisdom of finding an alternative living arrangement—I stayed with my family in what had been the CUSO volunteer's house. In this instance, CUSO's concern with obtaining as unbiased an evaluation as possible overcame the conflicting desire to allow Celia to play a central role in the evaluation project as a Melanesian woman.

Notes

1. Local people often invoked the wind as a factor to explain why they had sold little fish to Remre that month. This confused me, for often the fishermen who complained of high winds would brave rough seas if the price of fish rose or if they patched up their relationship with the manager. So I looked more seriously at what the fishermen meant by wind, and at sales of fish to Remre from canoes and motorboats.

In a sample of 1044 sales to Remre in 1985, 79 individuals sold 7,529 kg of fish for a total value of $7490. There was considerable monthly variation. For example, in July, Remre bought only 384 kg of fish from 23 sellers in 61 transactions. In April, however, the association purchased 1.7 tonnes of fish from 51 sellers in 284 transactions.

Obviously, when the fishing is good, more people go fishing. But the question of what makes the fishing good is not easy to answer. In April and October, high volume months, prime commercial species accounted for about half of the fish sold to Remre. But in July, a low volume month, mixed fish composed 61 percent of the association's purchases by weight. To catch snapper, a fisherman must venture into deep water; to catch mixed fish, he can stay inside the shelter of the reef.

At first glance, the pattern of species caught in high volume and low volume months suggests that weather is the crucial factor. July was a month of wind. Pekoa airfield near Luganville recorded 12 days with wind speeds greater than 12 knots for the month. But wind, as the Port Olry fishermen are quick to point out, is often an economic problem. If the economic incentive is sufficient, Port Olry boats will set to sea in a strong wind, but even a moderate wind will provide an excuse for staying in port if economic conditions seem unfavorable. Only one of the fishermen interviewed expressed any fear of going out in bad weather, an attitude remarkable in people with a reputation for being "fair weather fishermen" and for complaining that high winds often kept them from fishing. So it seems unlikely that the fact that there were 12 windy days in July accounts for the small number of premium fish caught.

In July 1984, Pekoa airport recorded 14 days of wind speeds greater than 12 knots, yet Remre bought 1.19 tonnes of fish (compared to 384 kg in July 1985). The fact that in July 1983, when there were 18 days of high winds, Remre purchased 3.642 tonnes of fish provides strong evidence that weather can be an excuse rather than an explanation for variations in the fishing effort.

Instead it seems likely that the low volume of fish and the high percentage of mixed fish in July 1985 indicates what kind of economic wind was blowing at the time. If fishermen do not think deep water fishing is worth their while financially, they confine their fishing to the shallow waters close to home. They use canoes which consume no expensive benzine and have no crew to be paid. They fish for subsistence and sell any incidental surplus. This surplus is likely to be small and to consist of mixed fish.

A comparison of data for July with October shows the relative preference for canoes over fishing boats in a low volume month. In July only 3 fishing boats were active, making up 13 percent of the fleet; their combined catch of 148 kg constituted 38 percent of the monthly total. In contrast, 13 fishing boats sold 1857 kg or 64 percent of the October total; in October, 31 percent of the fleet were fishing boats. Although canoes declined as a percentage of the fleet between July and October, there were actually more canoes fishing commercially in October, indicating an increased fishing effort for both canoe and boat fishermen.

2. The Luganville market is held three times a week. The women of Port Olry supply the market one weekday while the women of South Santo are responsible for the second weekday market. Both Port Olry and South Santo women combine their produce at the larger Saturday market.

3. The first seven years of missionary contact had resulted in not a single convert to Catholicism in Vanuatu (MacClancy 1981:73).

4. These villages include Loran, Lomo, Lovatkar, and Lorearokat. The settlement known as Corner, whose 150 or so residents I have not counted among the 600 residents of Port Olry, adjoins the main village. The residents of Corner come from Lotoror farther up Cap Queiros, and most of them maintain homes in both settlements.

5. A green bag contains the equivalent of roughly 30-35 kg of dried copra.

6. By comparison, in Ambae which is also a prosperous place relative to other locations in Vanuatu, two-thirds of the houses are made of traditional materials.

7. This is a rather large number of female-headed households. Perhaps the services of the mission attracted women without husbands to the community.

8. See Rodman and Rodman (1985) for a discussion of the relative power of traditional leaders, elected leaders and young voters in the context of renaming Ambae.

9. Missionaries introduced the shapeless cotton Mother Hubbard to Vanuatu, but islanders have appropriated the garment as the national dress, adding flounces, lace, and ribbons that flow from the sleeves and flutter in the slightest breeze.

9

MANAGING DEVELOPMENT IN PORT OLRY

Remre Fishing Association was officially created in December 1982. There were 36 original shareholders, each of whom purchased at least one $20 share. In contrast to a common practice in Melanesian companies of restricting members to a single share so that all start out as financial equals, some of the shareholders in Remre invested more money than others in the venture. Celia Sarsom, the woman who was so influential in organizing Remre, did not purchase any shares for herself; but she ensured that her husband Philip bought ten shares and that her father (the old chief Marcel) bought three. One of her father's strongest supporters, a planter of mixed French-Vanuatu heritage, also acquired 10 shares. Another close relative bought 7 shares. This meant that 4 people, all in Celia's sphere of influence controlled 30 shares in the association while the remaining 32 shareholders each held only one share apiece. And 14 of these shareholders were also close relatives of Celia's whom she could expect to side with her.

Few established fishermen bought shares in the association. Chief Marcel asked the planter to visit Port Olry residents and encourage them to buy shares in Remre. The planter told me that he had little success in doing as the chief requested; "It wasn't *hard* for people to buy shares. The problem was that they were not *happy* about buying shares." Too many local people remembered the losses they had already sustained by participating in previous maritime ventures. This was especially true for fishermen who had joined in the failed attempt to start an earlier fishing association.

But a lack of interest in purchasing shares in Remre in no way signified a lack of interest in fishing. Local fishermen were keen to learn new techniques for trolling and catching deep water snappers. Port Olry people generally are eager to explore new ways of earning money, and fishing had a particular appeal because it was an activity that a large number of men already enjoyed.

When Ken Ford and his wife Caroline arrived in Port Olry in January 1983, they found the people enthusiastic about the potential of fishing as a commercial activity. As a Village Fisheries Advisor, Ken Ford managed the fishing association. CUSO provided him with a 5.5 m Hartley fishing boat which he used to teach new fishing techniques and find new fishing grounds. Ken assisted local people to replace their canoes with small outboard-powered boats equipped with handreels. In February 1983 there were 35–40 fishermen using canoes in Port Olry. A year later, 5 commercial fishing boats had been purchased, and by 1985 there were 15 fishing boats on the village beach. Initially, he established a system of fish preservation, transport, and marketing using insulated containers and ice. Later he installed the walk-in coldroom for the association. Overall, he reduced the rate of fish spoilage from about 50 percent to 5 percent.

The capital cost of establishing the fishing association, including the coldroom, was $11,000. Remre raised $1,100 through the sale of shares as a personal contribution toward defraying capital costs. Government grants provided $5,500. Ken Ford ensured that the association's Development Bank loan of $4,400 representing the balance of the project's costs, was repaid before his departure. Moreover, he was able to pay shareholders a dividend of 30 percent, or $6 per share.

During the first year of operation, Remre Association marketed about 20 tonnes of fish and crustaceans, and showed a profit of $7,900 which was 18 percent of sales, or 40 cents per kg (see Table 3). The first flush of enthusiasm for a new project, virgin stocks of fish, and good weather contributed to the project's early success. But by 1985, estimated throughput had fallen off to about 12 tonnes per year; in a good month the profit margin was 5 percent of sales; the cost of buying fish from Port Olry fishermen had risen by about 10 percent of sales

TABLE 3

Remre Fishing Association Costs and Profit as a Percentage of Sales

	1983–84	1985
Cost of fish	60%	71%
Other expenses	22	30
Profit	18	(1)

revenue; and the association was showing a loss of $540 for the first ten months of the year.

Rapid repayment of the initial loan, exceptionally good fishing conditions, and a large dividend payment to shareholders while the CUSO cooperant was still in charge may have raised expectations, both in the village and in the Fisheries Department, regarding Remre's economic success. Since Ken Ford's departure, fishermen have been uncertain about the association's rate of profit, and the department has been concerned about Remre's financial decline. Part of my research in Port Olry involved a thorough assessment of Remre's financial situation.[1] The highlights of my findings appear as Appendix A.

Remre: The Manager's Garden?

Partly because of the fact that many fishermen were not involved as shareholders in Remre, and partly because of the deeper historical problems in the community, Ken Ford found that villagers were not very interested in running Remre Association as a local project. From the beginning Ken recognized that it would be difficult to transfer the management of the association to the local people; while they wanted the association to succeed, there was a general unwillingness to participate in the day to day running of Remre or to oversee its long-run planning.

The fact that the key shareholders in the association were the ruling minority in the village and that many fishermen were not shareholders clearly contributed to most people's lack of interest in helping to run the association. Except for the faction in which Celia was central, Port Olry people were wary of having anything to do with the government, a wariness that included fisheries development. Adamantly independent in their outlook, they wanted to be their own masters; they were enthusiastic about buying boats, but wanted no strings attached. It was very difficult for the Fisheries Department to compel their loyalty.

Some fishermen took advantage of Ken's connections with the Fisheries Department to obtain boats that were subsidized by grants and eligible for Development Bank loans. But other Port Olry fishermen remained uneasy about dealing with the government. They would rather pay cash for an aluminum skiff from a private seller, even if they had to pay far more than the cost of a boat obtained through the Fisheries Department. Some even preferred to buy fuel at private prices to avoid involvement with the Fisheries Department.

One fisherman who bought a used boat and motor with a loan for

$1600 from Barclay's Bank explained to me that he wanted to be a private business man and retain the right to sell his fish to whomever he wished. He bought his boat without going through the Fisheries Department because he wanted it to be *his own* boat. Consequently, he felt under no obligation to deal with the Fisheries Department and thought that the department had no right to prevent fishermen from finding other markets.

This man, and one or two others like him, bought fish in Port Olry which they sold to private buyers in Luganville. At first he also sold to the government outlet Santofish, but the Fisheries Department soon required that Santofish refuse to buy from this man because he was competing with Remre, thereby undermining the fishing association. To this man, and to others in Port Olry, competition seemed a natural part of free enterprise rather than a blow struck against Remre, but the Fisheries Department disagreed.

In October 1983, Remre's executive committee selected Manuel, Chief Marcel's son, to become the manager of Remre gradually taking Ken's place during the final year of the CUSO volunteer's contract. Many Port Olry people were dissatisfied with the selection process whereby Manuel became manager. The executive committee consisted of five shareholders, but the chief was invited to join the committee in order to help choose the manager. In the end, it was Chief Marcel who cast the deciding vote, selecting his own son, Manuel, to become Remre's manager. Following Marcel's death in 1984, Manuel was elected to the office of village chief; he continued to manage the fishing association.

Popular opposition to Manuel was widespread from the day he was selected as manager of Remre. He was criticized for paying too low a price for fish, for being unavailable to buy fish during working hours, for changing fish prices capriciously, for failing to use a bank for Remre's money, and for an ever-changing range of other alleged misdeeds. To some, Remre seemed to be simply "the Manager's garden" from which he could harvest at will.

But Manuel is clever and tenacious. His critics were unable to remove him from his position as manager. They could not prove that he was less than honest. Audits of Remre's books indicated that all was in order. Manuel was able to turn to Celia and the Fisheries Department for the support he needed to maintain his position in the community. When the fishermen went on strike, or sold fish to another local buyer, or demanded that Manuel be replaced, the Fisheries Department strategy was to send an expatriate employee up to Port Olry to straighten things out. The expatriate spoke with "key people" in Port Olry, who were scattered throughout the village, but who were all men on whom Celia Sarsom could count for support.

When local fishermen feel they can no longer deal with Manuel, for social or economic reasons, their characteristic response has been to go on strike, ceasing to fish commercially although they continue to catch fish from canoes for personal consumption. This practice has puzzled and frustrated government and development workers who try to figure out what the local fishermen are on strike *for*. The key to understanding this situation is to realize that this is not a question of being on strike *for* anything, but of opting out until conditions improve.

A Fisheries Department officer or a volunteer may encourage people who are on strike to resume commercial fishing. This is frequently achieved by sending a fisheries officer to the area in question; in Port Olry in 1985, the idea was for the officer to support Manuel's authority as manager of the association and to catch large numbers of fish, creating local enthusiasm through a demonstration effect. In other words, as one officer put it, "The idea is to get them all hepped up." But this, as both the Port Olry people and the Fisheries Department recognize, is usually a temporary rather than a viable long-term solution. A more effective strategy is to ask *why* people don't want to fish, don't want to meet to discuss the fishing association, or don't want to sell fish to Remre. Going on strike was virtually the only collective action that I observed among the strong individualists of Port Olry. Striking in this way is not irrational; it is an effective means of coping that should signal to the government that a real problem exists. The source of the problem generally could be found by talking at length to the people on strike, rather than to those they seem to be striking against; but to the Fisheries Department this has seemed time-consuming and tedious.

The Price Is the Captain:
Fishing for the Market

It is clear that fresh fish was an important food item in Port Olry before the fishing project began. Commercial fishing has probably increased the amount of fish in the diet because fishermen generally hold some of their catch aside for consumption. But this increase is not significant simply because, by and large, Port Olry people were already consuming as much fish as they wanted.

I found that, overall, most households eat fish at least three times a week. Many residents prefer fresh fish to fresh beef because of taste and texture. Fish is also popular because most families can catch their own, unlike beef which must be purchased at the Boucherie de Brousse for about $1/kg.

Some people who have recently moved to Port Olry from the Santo bush, as well as a few older residents of the village never eat fish, because they follow a tabu that forbids them to eat fresh fish or come in contact with saltwater. I found it interesting that the tabu never extended to tinned fish, which seems further evidence for regarding tinned and fresh fish as conceptually different kinds of food.

Since almost every family that eats fish can catch its own free, fresh fish, Remre can sell only a small amount of its product locally. Moreover, the association faces a small amount of competition for this limited market from fishermen who sell their catch informally on the beach. All fishermen are expected to sell their catch to Remre, but a few feel no sense of obligation to do so, while others will sell their fish on the beach occasionally if the manager of the fishing association is not available to buy their catch before it spoils.

Still, Remre has improved access to fresh fish for those who, although not numerous, are the most in need: the 14 percent of the households in the research population that are headed by single women. These women are widows, unwed mothers, or women who live separately from their husbands. Unless there is a boy in the household who is big enough to catch fish for the family, the women can only depend on the generosity of relatives who might share their catch. Women themselves, I was told, never go fishing on their own although they might accompany their husbands.[2] Single women who are household heads have little money to spend on food and they recognize that fresh fish offers good food value for a reasonable price (about $1/kg). Remre offers a convenient, regular source of fresh fish that these women in particular appreciate.

Although commercial species are popular for local consumption in other Village Fisheries Development projects, this is not the case in Port Olry. Some of the appeal of snapper no doubt lies in its novelty to islanders who have never before fished in deep enough water to catch these species. In Port Olry, men were tying 10 or 12 coils of fishing line together and catching snappers from their canoes before the development project even began.[3] For them, the novelty had worn off and they did not consider snapper to be a good eating fish. To many Port Olry fishermen, if snappers were not saleable, they would be "fis blon sakemaot," fish to be thrown back in the sea. Some Port Olry people commented that they *did* like the "deepness" of the big snappers, by which they mean the thickness of the flesh, not the depth of the sea from which the fish comes; but they still said that poulet does not taste like "real" fish. The lack of a fishy taste that makes snappers popular with restaurant clientele is considered a drawback among these fishermen. Snapper is said to be "cold" and flavorless unless one adds a great deal of salt. The most popular species for local consumption are red mouth, big eye, and *mangru*.

The Port Olry project differs from others in the VFDP in that the goal was not to develop greater interest in fishing, per se, since fishing was already a well-established subsistence activity and commercial participation in fishing had already begun on a small scale using canoes. The project aimed at developing this commercial potential by encouraging fishermen to invest in motorboats and by providing them with a local market for deep water snappers.

Port Olry people like the idea of a fishing association that provides them with a local market because commercial fishing can be combined with other work. Fishing provides a way of earning money that supplements local people's incomes from copra and other sources. As elsewhere in Vanuatu, no one in Port Olry is a full-time fisherman. One of the attractions of fishing is precisely that a man can earn money *without* having to catch a lot of fish. As one fisherman said to me, "We can use Remre along with copra, cocoa and cattle. Fishing is not as hard work as making copra. It is easy to earn $40–60 from fish, but it is not profitable to make just a little copra."

The people of Port Olry earned approximately $390,000 from sales of copra, cattle, cocoa, and fish in 1985. Copra provided by far the largest single source of income, about $331,000 in 1985, or $1,230 per seller.[4] Cattle sales yielded about $34,500 for Port Olry breeders. Fish sales to Remre, at about $18,000 in 1985, are the third largest source of income for which data are available. Cocoa provides villagers with about $5,000 annually. In 1985, $17,000 in reparations payments were paid to 33 Port Olry people for damages incurred in the 1980 rebellion. Data for sales of garden produce at the Luganville market, for truck-taxi incomes, and for store sales were not available, but these sources of income would add at least another $100,000 annually. Thus, the total estimated income for the village of about 600 people is more than $500,000 per year (see Table 4).

TABLE 4
Sources of Income for Port Olry Village (population approx. 600), 1985

Copra	$331,000
Cattle	34,500
Fish	18,000
Cocoa	5,000
Reparations	17,000
Market, taxi, stores—estimate	100,000
TOTAL	$505,500

Fishing is not a primary source of income. All but 3 Port Olry fishermen earned more money from copra than they did from fish in 1985. Copra, even at half the 1985 price of $360 per tonne, would have earned a man $75 per working week.[5] In comparison, among those who sold fish to Remre, the average individual's income from fishing was only about $227 in 1985, or pro-rated over a 40-week working year, a mere $5.68 per working week. Of the 79 men who sold fish to Remre in my sample of 1044 cases, only 4 earned incomes of more than $1000 per year from fish.

The average income from fishing boats was considerably greater than the average fisherman's income, which takes into account canoes as well as motorized boats. Fishing boats provided about two-thirds of Remre's volume. Income for each of 13 fishing boats in 1985 came to $922. Most boats' earnings go to a variety of captains and crew, as well as to the owner. Canoe fishermen supplied about one-third of Remre's total fish purchases; assuming 29 canoes, the average income per canoe would be about $207. Income per fisherman would be lower than this because more than one person usually has the right to use a particular canoe.

Clearly, fishermen were also earning money from other activities. Nevertheless, fishing provides a more important source of income for fishermen than any productive activity except copra. Further, fishing may prove to be a more important source of income when copra prices are low.[6]

Ken Ford had a clear understanding of the Port Olry people's motivation regarding Remre. I met with him in Canada before I began my research. When I asked him why the local people wanted a VFDP project, he replied, "Their main objective was money." I asked him if he meant money earned from fish or money received as aid. "Money from fish," Ken explained, "The aid is not so obvious because no cash goes to the recipient. People can see that a locally produced boat obtained through Fisheries is cheaper than a private import, but they may not realize that the difference is because of aid money. What the Port Olry people wanted was cash from fish to supplement copra and market garden incomes."

One Port Olry person expressed this view of the place of fishing in the allocation of his labor time succinctly and, I thought, rather poetically. In the words of this canoe fisherman, the captain makes the decision to go fishing, and in Port Olry "the price of fish is the captain."

Ken Ford felt that his greatest contribution was in serving as an effective middleman linking Port Olry fishermen to the larger world of government and business. He knew that local people were capable of a massive fishing effort for the market if the price was right. For example, in April 1984, the Port Olry fishermen were happy to fulfill David Shepherd's request to catch a tonne of white poulet fish using the *iki jimi* method for export to Britain.[7] The fishermen have never forgotten that they received an especially high price for that fish and that it was sent directly from Port Olry to Port Vila, bypassing the Santofish market.

One of Ken's biggest difficulties in his middleman role was running interference between the Fisheries Department which sought to deepen Port Olry fishermen's linkages with the marketplace and fishermen who sought the best price for their fish, preferred a free market, and were proud of whatever independence they could maintain from the government. The Fisheries Department has insisted that all Port Olry fish be sold to Remre, which in turn must sell all of its fish to Port Vila Fisheries' market in Santo; but this rule has been impossible to enforce.[8] Port Olry fishermen need a market for their fish; so long as markets sponsored by the Fisheries Department—i.e., Remre and Santofish—could ensure that theirs was the only chain of markets available to Port Olry people, the government could compel the villagers' loyalty. But the Port Olry people have always been on the lookout for ways to circumvent this situation.

In part, the endless search for a way around selling fish directly to Remre has been a protest against Manuel's management of the fishing association. During periods when he was often unavailable, when he did not pay captains as soon as they sold him their catch, or when he was suspected of finagling the price of fish, local people preferred to sell their fish elsewhere, or to stop fishing commercially.

But Manuel, too, was eager to find new buyers for Remre's fish who would offer him a more favorable price than Santofish. Manuel acknowledged that he sometimes sold fish to Chinese buyers in Luganville who would offer as much as $1 more per kg for mixed, non-premium species than Santofish would pay him. But he could not count on selling to the Chinese because their freezers were fairly small; unlike Port Vila Fisheries, these firms were under no obligation to buy all fish of good quality, and their demand for Port Olry fish was consequently erratic and limited.

Ken also found the marketing situation frustrating. He sought to obtain the best price he could for Port Olry fishermen, while supporting the Fisheries Department and Port Vila Fisheries. He felt the Port Olry fishermen deserved a more consistent policy concerning pricing and fish handling. Ford repeatedly complained that the fishermen were told to prepare fish using the *iki jimi* technique one week, while the two weeks later they were expected to gut and clean all the fish instead of keeping it whole. And Ford questioned the markup at Port Vila Fisheries, wondering why it was that the fish market in Port Vila seemed to make a profit of 70 to 90 cents a kg while the Port Olry fishermen received only 50 to 80 cents a kg.

Most of all, Ford objected to the inconsistency in the fish markets' entreaties to Remre to catch more fish for the market at some times and to stop commercial fishing altogether at other times. Despite Port Vila Fisheries' claim that it would buy all the fish islanders could supply, informal quotas were imposed in times of peak production, such as the early months of 1984 and 1986. Fishermen were asked not to fish, although the fish markets allegedly would continue to buy any fish that was brought to them. Of course, Ford was well-aware that these contradictory orders stemmed from the problems of over and under-supply that have been part of the process of establishing markets for fish in Vanuatu. But he also could see that Port Olry fishermen resented such inconsistency and that their opposition to Port Vila Fisheries policies contributed to the frequency with which they went on strike.

The Social Dynamics of Development

Despite these difficulties, sales of fish to Remre Association have provided a source of income for fishermen who range from children to old men, from those who catch 100 kg of premium snapper to those who catch a netful of sardines. Some of the most frequently cited benefits of the association are that 1) payment is made in the village—one doesn't have to go to Luganville to sell the commodity as is the case with copra, 2) payment is immediate, and 3) even a small fishing effort from a canoe can yield a cash income.

Fishermen have found that, with hard work and luck, they can earn enough money fishing to achieve their development goals. While some have been boat owners, the benefits of the project have reached canoe fishermen as well as those with the money to buy or operate boats. One older man who fished only from a canoe within the lagoon earned enough money from sales of fish, especially *mangru*, to buy a piece of land and hire laborers to clear and plant it in coconuts. The fisherman named the new plantation "Mangru" after the species which made it possible.

Ken had mixed feelings about encouraging fishermen to replace their canoes with outboard motor boats. While he hoped for success stories such as the canoe fisherman who created "Mangru Plantation," he felt that most fishermen would like to move up to fishing boats. But, compared to canoes, fishing boats are expensive, not just to buy but also to maintain. Although Port Olry men would catch more fish from the boats they would have to spend more money to achieve those larger catches. Ken wasn't sure if this was a good idea.

Ken need not have worried that fishermen would replace their canoes with motorboats. There were 29 canoes in use in Port Olry when I was there. Most subsistence fishing continues to be done from canoes on a daily basis because these vessels are convenient and cost nothing to operate. The availability of both fishing boats and canoes have provided village fishermen with new options to fish commercially or to feed the family. They also allow local people to withdraw from commercial fishing without ceasing to fish for food.

As far as the villagers were concerned, Remre ran smoothly so long as Ken was in charge. While several people told me pointedly that Ken had not taught one person in Port Olry to fish, since they were already able to catch deep water snappers, they did find that they could learn from him. Ken developed effective methods for transferring his knowledge without seeming to teach. He tried to show individuals or small groups how to do something rather than explaining the task in the abstract. He found that a new technique would catch on much more quickly if he could get one Port Olry man to use it rather than using it himself.

Another volunteer who had returned to Canada stressed to me that the role of the advisor in the success of any VFDP project should not be underestimated. I questioned him further on this point:

Q: So it's a question of how well the advisor relates to the local people?

A: Yeah, in terms of being patient, understanding, non-assertive. You always have to turn the question around so *they* are asking *you* what *you* want to ask *them*, and they know the answer. You have to give them the answer and then get them to ask you the question. It takes a certain type of person to do that well. When you have that type of person, you have successful projects.

The local people aren't perfect either, but a poor advisor will dwell on their bad points instead of picking up their good points, and the project fails, whereas a good advisor overlooks the bad points, works to overcome them and emphasizes the good points.

Q: Can you give me an example of how you give the local person the answer, then get them to ask the question?

A: At Port Olry, when they started fishing using their boats with the engines, it became obvious that there were other areas that would have more fish because no one had ever fished there. Now you can't say, "Okay everyone. Let's all get our boats together and go over behind

Sakao Island and fish there. You have to get the people to come up with it.

So you have to say to the people, "Do you think there would be any fish behind Sakao Island?" And, "Do you think it would be a good idea if I went over there and tried fishing?" Then you come back from fishing there and say, "Gee, that was a good idea you had!" You sort of put the words in their mouth. All the time you wanted to go over there and fish, but you make them think that it's because you spoke to them that you went. You're instilling confidence in them. It's like that with everything. You're getting them to sanction what you do, then you give them the credit.

Q: What if the fishing trip doesn't work out well?

A: Well, the people are basically non-confrontational. But you don't come back and say they're wrong!

Working in this way, Ken was able to encourage many Port Olry fishermen to catch deep water snappers for the market using their new boats. He wondered what the social consequences of this development would be on the community. Would it be like the orange project on the island of Aniwa in southern Vanuatu where, as one volunteer put it, "everybody sold oranges, made money, bought beer, and beat up on their families"? When I visited Port Olry about a year after the Fords had left, I found that in some ways the new boats had encouraged social differentiation, but in other ways the benefits of the project had been broadly distributed throughout the community.

Fishing boats generally had a single owner, and often the owner was a man who was already fairly wealthy by local standards. A fishing boat provided an investment opportunity for people who had made money from copra, for example, in a situation where such opportunities are still rare. But purchase of a boat did not mean the owner had to go out on the sea in it. In fact, 5 of the 15 owners of fishing boats in Port Olry never went fishing. Nine others hired captains for their boats part of the time. Only one man always served as the captain of his own boat.

Some boat owners who are not fishermen acquired their boats, or outfitted them for fishing, specifically to provide employment for family members. Such behavior conforms with Melanesian social expectations that wealthier individuals should help their poorer relatives to earn money, thereby levelling income inequalities to some extent and minimizing jealousy of those who are more affluent. In Port Olry as in Longana, it is customary for influential men to express concern about providing younger men in the community with opportunities for achievement. The purchase of a fishing boat is often justified in these terms, and indeed crewing on the boats is a very popular activity among the young men of Port Olry.

It is not unusual for a boat to have a purchaser, an owner, a captain, and several crew. For example, one fishing boat whose history I traced was purchased at the time of Ken Ford's departure in late 1984 by a carpenter who works in Luganville but spends the weekends in his home in Port Olry.[9] The carpenter's brother, Henri, had asked him to buy the boat so that he could try his hand at commercial fishing.[10] Henri was enthusiastic about the idea of fishing, he told me, because it seemed to him to provide a good opportunity to earn money fairly easily. But he only went fishing once in the boat his brother bought him. He says he stayed out on the water all day and filled his insulated fish box, but he found that day that fishing was not something he really enjoyed doing. Subsequently his sons took the boat out a few times, but none of them developed into serious fishermen.

Soon Camille, whom Port Olry people agree is one of the best fishermen in the area, let Henri know that he would be interested in becoming the captain of Henri's blue boat. Although Camille has an aptitude for fishing combined with years of experience fishing from canoes and considerable training in deep water techniques, he has never been able to afford his own boat.

I greeted Camille one day as he came ashore from an overnight fishing trip. Canoe fishermen and some captains of fishing boats prefer to fish in groups, partly in order to keep a look out for whales which, it is believed, might endanger the small boats, but Camille likes to fish away from other boats. He is not afraid of the sea and told of once singlehandedly killing a shark that was bigger than his boat.

On this occasion, he and one crew had returned from fishing behind Sakao Island. He had slept on the beach there for a few hours, then fished throughout the night. Although there is a fish aggregating device in place far out on the Port Olry bank, Camille did not go there. Not only was the sea rough, but he had been discouraged by his last trip to the raft when he used $10 in fuel and caught only one mahimahi, from which a shark took a large chunk. On this trip behind Sakao he had caught about 15 kg of premium fish. One fish was held aside for the chief of the village of Corner where Camille lived; Camille kept 4 small fish for his own household. He doesn't like the taste of big fish, he told me, only small ones.

Port Olry fishermen, unlike fishermen involved in smaller VFDP projects, are expected to carry ice for fish preservation, even when they fish from canoes. Ideally the ratio of ice to fish is 1:1. Camille had taken a 20 kg block of ice with him when he left the previous evening to go fishing. Like all Port Olry fishermen, he obtained the ice from

Manuel, who bought it at the South Pacific Fishing Company where prices were cheaper than Santofish. Manuel let Camille take the ice, which cost $2, on credit and would deduct the cost from the value of the catch. With fishermen who he was less certain would return with fish to sell to Remre, Manuel demanded cash payment.

Camille's ice had melted by the time he returned home. Rather than carry the ice-chest all the way from the river landing to his house, a distance of half a kilometer, Camille removed the fish from the cold water in the chest and carried them up to his house, strung on bits of bush-rope. As soon as Camille reached his house, his wife went to look for a truck to take the fish to Remre. But the truck took an hour to arrive. As I sat talking with Camille, I could see the quality of the fish, which Camille had hung in the branches of the tree above our heads, deteriorate before my eyes. I remembered the manager of Port Vila Fisheries telling me that for every hour that fish is held at temperatures above 6° C it ages 16 hours. The temperature on this hot, sunny day was about 28°. As we waited for the truck and conversation lagged, I amused myself by trying to figure out, without much success, how much the fish was aging per second as I watched it hang in the tree. I also remembered the observation that the wise old man who is the ni-Vanuatu expert on *iki jimi* technique made about Port Olry fishermen; "They know how to catch fish, but they don't know how to keep it."

Manuel bought Camille's fish. It was not Camille's fault that the truck was so slow to arrive, and Manuel felt that he could not refuse to buy fish from one of his most loyal suppliers. But Manuel wasn't sure the fish would be acceptable to Santofish, which pays according to three grades of fish: A, B, and C. The manager of Port Vila Fisheries says "C" really stands for "sea," as in "throw it back in the sea." Manuel knew he would not make any money on the fish because the price he paid to the fishermen was set high enough that he lost money on any fish that Santofish graded lower than "A."

Port Olry fishermen use a rule of thumb that they call the "rule of quarters" to calculate the distribution of earnings from a fishing trip. Either one-quarter of the gross income is held aside "for the boat"— i.e., to cover operating costs or, less often, the actual costs are deducted from gross income. The remainder is divided into "three quarters"—one for the owner, one for the captain, and one for the crew. If the owner is also the captain, the crew's share may be increased to one-third of the gross. According to the rule of quarters, the owner, captain, and crew would each earn almost $7 from a 30 kg catch.

The day that I sat with Camille watching his fish swing from the branches and waiting for the truck, he had returned from fishing with his sister's son, Jean-Claude, as crew. Young men like Jean-Claude enjoy working as crew on the fishing boats partly because they are often paid the same rate as the captain. The captain is accorded deference, respect, and obedience; he is entrusted with making the decisions about when and where to fish; and he is usually responsible for gutting and selling the fish.[11] Yet he is expected to receive no greater share than his crew. The assumption underlying this practice is that if the captain were paid more, the crew would be jealous and would no longer want to go fishing. Boatowners who are also captains can set aside a portion of the sales income for "the boat," but it is not socially acceptable for them to appear to take a larger share of the balance for themselves than they pay to their crew.

The man who makes his own copra or operates his own fishing boat has the potential to earn more money than a crew member or a worker on a plantation. Yet for those who crew or make other people's copra, the choices about how to invest one's labour time are wider and more equivalent. A man who can earn about $8 per day cutting copra as a wage laborer may be willing to settle for the $6.50 or so he can earn from an ordinary fishing trip because he welcomes the opportunity to vary his work and because commercial fishing offers the possibility of catching far more than 30 kg in a lucky day. Moreover, a man can earn approximately the same amount fishing alone in his canoe: about $7/day according to Ken Ford's records from 1984. Thus, commercial fishing seems to have provided the widest range of options for the young men of Port Olry who serve as crew members on the fishing boats and as canoe fishermen in their own right.

Notes

1. This assessment appeared as a report on Remre Fishing Association (M. Rodman 1986) which I submitted to CUSO in February 1986.

2. I never saw or heard any evidence to the contrary while I was in Port Olry, although I am aware that the importance of women in fishing, especially from the shore or in shallow water, is often underestimated in Pacific research (Ifeka 1986; Schoeffel 1985).

3. Each coil contains 25 meters of fishing line.

4. Copra prices were relatively high for the first 3 years after the Commodities Marketing Board began to stabilize copra prices to local producers in 1982. However, the price of copra, which was $360 per tonne at the beginning of my study had dropped to only $130 per tonne by June 1986, so the relative contribution of copra to overall earnings in Port Olry may be quite different for 1986.

5. Copra prices fluctuate widely on the world market. For example, a tonne of copra fetched $320 in July 1987, but was worth only $150 a year earlier (ANZ Bank economic indicators in *Pacific Islands Monthly*, August 1987:27). The

copra marketing board in Vanuatu cushions these price fluctuations for producers in the islands.

6. Cocoa yielded a small income for 28 fishermen, but none earned more than $270 per annum from this commodity. Only 3 fishermen, and one boat owner who did not fish, earned money from the sale of cattle in 1985. For the fishermen this amounted to about $150 each. 13 boat owners and fishermen received reparations payments totalling $2,282, or an average of $176 apiece.

7. Port Olry fishermen learned the *iki jimi* technique for killing fish with a stab to the brain from a ni-Vanuatu expert who ran a training course on *iki jimi* for two weeks in the village.

8. During the five weeks I spent in Port Olry, fishermen went around to Big Bay on several occasions when they were "on strike" against Remre. They sold the fish they caught in Big Bay to a Fisheries Department Landrover that, at least at first, was unaware that these were Port Olry fishermen far from home.

9. Only 28 Port Olry residents work in Luganville; most maintain weekend homes in the village. There seems to be no problem with urban drift, largely because Port Olry is such a physically easy and pleasant place to live. I could find no one from Port Olry known to be unemployed and living in Luganville.

10. At Ken's suggestion, the carpenter went to the Fisheries Department in Santo to inquire about buying a boat. There he was urged to take out a Development Bank loan, but the carpenter resisted. He preferred always to pay cash for his purchases. He was not obliged to borrow from the Development Bank, the Fisheries Officer assured him, so the carpenter paid for his boat with a satchel full of $10 notes. The blue, wooden 5 m boat cost $850 secondhand. Fishing gear for the boat cost about $250. I am not sure how much the carpenter paid for the 16 hp outboard that had been on Ken Ford's fishing boat.

11. The question of the captain's authority is one that intrigued the CUSO volunteers, some of whom felt that it was difficult for ni-Vanuatu who tend to be non-confrontational in their social interaction to accept the authority that a captain needed. A CUSO couple cited the following examples of the problems captains encountered:

CUSO 1: One of the 6 captains [for the boat on the project where I worked] was a pretty good guy, very steady. His name was Big Bel. He had the second biggest month of any of the captains, ever. He did really well, and then he disappeared. Finally, when we needed a captain, I suggested Big Bel, but no the chairman of the committee said, "Oh, ol boy oli no wantem wok wetem hem" (None of the boys want to work with him). The reason was that all he did as captain was to run the boat and fish his reel. In other words, he did everything that a captain would do: he'd run the boat, decide where to go, tell the crew what to do, catch lots of fish, decide when to leave. They would catch fish and make money with them; but he would say, "Gut the fish!" and they didn't like that. They said he was too bossy because he told them what to do.

I said, "You say he's too bossy but he's the captain. And you guys make more money with him than you do with any of these other jerks that take the boat out." But they just didn't want to be *told* what to do. That's our theory.

CUSO 2: There was another guy we just loved. He came ashore one time and said, "I'm not going out with these guys anymore. They're my wife's relatives and they just don't take orders from me. I'm not allowed to swear in front of them or I'll get fined. And I can't give them orders because they're her family, so I just can't go out with these people." The issue wasn't the fact that one of the crew was a former MP, that didn't matter at all. That was a really different reason from what I expected!

10

CONCLUSION:
CONSTRAINTS AND OPTIONS

Far out on the horizon of an island and ocean world, the captain of a small boat casts lead weights into the sea. He must find his depth, casting again and again, sounding the bottom that he cannot see. In order to get to the bottom of the Village Fisheries Development Program, like a fisherman I too have sounded its depths, dropping a line here, a weight there, moving on, probing again. As any village fisherman knows, deep water alone does not provide a home for the red snapper that he seeks. The snapper's milieu is a small niche created where the reef meets the deep sea, a milieu that is the product of the island and the Pacific but that is, in itself, neither land nor open ocean. Just as the snapper exists where the land's edge meets the sea's depth, so village fisheries development in Vanuatu is a product of particular contradictory forces that meet beneath the surface.

VFDP and Domestic Policy

Vanuatu's Village Fisheries Development Program (VFDP) has been the "golden apple in the basket" of development programs, to quote the Director of the Fisheries Department; the VFDP has attracted the attention of aid donors, volunteer organizations, and planners in governments throughout the region. The VFDP has particular appeal to the state in Vanuatu for domestic policy reasons.

First, the nearly 100 VFDP projects established in Vanuatu by the end of 1985 seem to provide a way to increase productive activity in the rural sector; in other words, the VFDP encourages islanders to make money and to operate small businesses. While the government recognizes that commercial fishing is likely to be a sporadic activity, according to well-established island patterns, the VFDP is part of a general attempt to educate rural people about the need for increased productivity. More "productive projects" are required in the rural areas to generate cash to pay the fees and taxes that will cover the cost of government services. A constituency in which people cut copra only when they need money to pay school fees or to cover the expenses associated with the delivery of a child requires more than new ways to make money. A radical change in peoples' attitudes toward money, work, and government is required to transform intermittent simple commodity producers into people who work regularly to provide the money that creates the tax base to keep local government running.[1] Such a transformation will not occur through the VFDP alone, and most projects are likely to be disappointing to the government in terms of productive activity. Yet the VFDP seems to be one step, however small, toward the goal of increased rural productivity.

Second, the VFDP provides an investment opportunity for islanders who have made money from copra or other sources. Previously, rural entrepreneurs found there was little they could do with their money except invest in social relationships or acquire items from a limited range of available consumer goods. The VFDP is particularly attractive because it offers local people a way to invest their money not just in boats but in people. Both the Longana and Port Olry cases illustrate that some entrepreneurs explain their investment in boats explicitly in terms of "helping others." Traditionally, leaders exhibit an ability to draw both people and objects of wealth to their sides; entrepreneurs who procure boats through the VFDP help themselves while giving their community access to fresh fish (in the case of Longana) and making it possible for young men in the community to find employment fishing.[2]

Was the Longana Fishing Project
a Success?

Financial prosperity is not the only criterion by which to evaluate the success of a VFDP project. In Longana, the project's manager succeeded in consuming a development project as if it were a truck he bought and drove into the ground or a bag of rice he used up at a feast. He mined the potential of that project to increase his personal standing in the community. In the end, this act of consumption did little or nothing to increase his prestige or to improve the quality of life in the community, but the failure of the project in this sense was simply a failure to transform an act of consumption into a social asset.

Soon after I left, a new CUSO cooperant was posted to Lolowai. He and his family moved into the Fisheries house that Tom had built with Jackers Company beside Lolowai Bay. The new cooperant was to serve for two years as one of the first Fisheries Department Extension Officers, working in conjunction with the Local Government headquarters at Saraitamata. Rather than being tied to a specific project, as Tom had been linked to Jackers, the extension officer would serve as a resource person, a "travelling helper" based at Lolowai but available to assist people throughout the local government area who wanted to learn more about deep water fishing. The introduction of extension officers offered a solution to the problem of ensuring that those with the greatest need and the strongest interest in fishing can obtain assistance when they want it. Individuals with Silas's entrepreneurial bent and experience in dealing with outsiders often have been able to obtain projects before less assertive villagers. A resident extension officer will be available for local people—women as well as men—who seek him out, rather than appearing to be the property of any particular project.

The Longana people with whom I spoke regarded Jackers Company with skepticism. There was some jealousy of Silas's ability to obtain the Fisheries Department's support for the project. In 1982, we had gone to Port Vila with one of our Longana neighbors who wanted to start a fishing project in Lolowai, but Silas's company was already in the process of formation and the department was unwilling to consider a second project in the area until the first one had proved itself. It was clear to the islanders that Silas had no real interest in fishing, but this would not have mattered if the project had provided a regular source of fresh fish, or if Silas had been able to forge the young boys under his authority into an effective work group. Because he has been unable to do either of these things, Silas's fishing project has not given him the new prestige in the community he had hoped for. The local people felt that they had yet to benefit from the fishing project, although the presence of a Fisheries Extension Officer, which might not have occurred without the Jackers project, promises to more widely distribute both the access to fishing projects and the benefits from them.

In designing my research on fisheries development, I was particularly curious to see how the Jackers project would compare with copra-making, which is the predominant form of simple commodity production in Vanuatu. At first I was disappointed to learn that Jackers was operating on a very small scale in terms of its volume of business. Because the Fisheries Department had to limit the number of projects in the area, the wealthier men who might have diversified their business activities did not invest in fishing; neither could people who had little access to copra move into fishing as a source of income so long as Jackers was the focus for fisheries development in the area. Basically, the project seemed not to improve the quality of life in Longana, but its social costs were minor. Only those households which had sons working as crew members experienced any direct impact from the project; these households received no benefits in terms of fish, and little if any remittances from their sons' meager wages; to them the cost of the fishing project was their sons' unhappy experience at what was for many a first job.

Yet the more I considered the place of deep water fishing in Longana, the more it seemed to me that I was wrong to think that such a project as Jackers makes no difference. The difference it makes is one of potential, the potential for commercial fishing activity. When I left, Jackers was facing a crisis; the company could not afford to buy the drum of fuel St. Peter's Star needed to go fishing. But I would not be surprised if Jackers emerged from that crisis and once again caught as much as $700 worth of fish per month. *For a while.* This is not a criticism, merely a way of saying that fish is likely to be incorporated into rural lifestyles as just another cash-crop, albeit one that is hunted not grown.[3]

Islanders display a passive resistance to commercialization of their labor. Capital investment and expert training will not transform Longanans into full-time fishermen because there are other social demands that compete for their labor.[4] Even successful commercial fishermen in Canada don't fish all the time.[5] So while Jackers was clearly beset with problems—including personality conflicts between Silas, Tom, and David Shepherd, three very strong-willed people—it has as much potential as other fishing projects in Vanuatu for satisfying local criteria of success. By the same token, it has almost no chance of becoming a thriving business in the capitalist sense.

What is happening on Ambae is similar to what those involved in fisheries development are finding elsewhere in rural Vanuatu. Experienced CUSO volunteers recognize that fisheries projects can be consistent with most islanders' desire to work intermittently for cash, as the following exchange between two volunteers indicates:

CUSO 1. Any project here is going to be sporadic. There's going to be times when they get all hepped up, go out fishing, and maybe catch lots of fish for a month at a time. Then it will peter out, the enthusiasm will die out, the boat will 'sleep'; but it's okay because they have other sources of income—they'll cut copra, look after their gardens. *Nobody can be a full-time anything!* And also it's part of their lifestyle too; they've got to have time just to hang out under the banyan tree.

If they keep the boat there it will work its way into their lifestyle. It will be part-time fishing, but it will be "fasin blon olgeta" (their way of doing things).

CUSO 2. I don't think that's wrong. Why adopt all those things that give them heart attacks. I don't think we should be trying to achieve anything that's disconnected from what *they* want to achieve, because that's what we came here for.

Silas found that even dealing with Jackers could be a headache. He said he didn't think he would take on another development project. He might be willing to help someone else start his own project; "After all," he said with a smile, "I do have a little knowledge about how to deal with the government." But Silas felt that if he himself undertook another development project he would worry too much. "It wouldn't be good to worry myself to death over these projects. I am afraid it might kill me. Even now if the boys are not working well, I worry a lot, and I know that if I keep on worrying like that I'll have a heart attack."

Clearly, the greater an islander's investment in a fishing project and the greater his loan burden, the more he is likely to worry. The Fisheries Department has recognized that projects, such as Jackers, that were oriented around the Alia catamarans were too large scale for Vanuatu village conditions. The smaller Hartley-design boats are better suited to part-time fishing. Even so, the Fisheries Department finds the temptation to increase capital investment in fishing projects hard to resist. Aid donors prefer to support the purchase of capital equipment than to cover services which are less tangible. Village fishermen often ask for equipment that they hope will bring prosperity to their projects. A technological solution, such as the freezer for Jackers Fishing Company offers a deceptively easy response to what the department realizes may be a complex social problem; yet is the response that the department often employs as a temporary panacea. Although the department displays considerable interest in canoe modernization and in fisheries development on a small scale, the department distributes a lot of western technology, a lot of "cargo" in the islands.

There is cargo in the breeze that sifts the papers and slams the doors in the Port Vila Fisheries Department. This is particularly true for projects larger than Jackers, although Silas's project was obviously overcapitalized. Projects the size of the Port Olry Fishing Association are the direction in which most of the cargo blows. Freezers and bigger boats, icemakers and Landrovers, all find their way into village fishing projects making it possible for small projects to consume development on a larger scale and encouraging them to increase their fishing effort, but also making it uneconomic for villagers to leave the boat on the beach when they would like to do something other than go fishing.

Was the Port Olry Fishing Project a Success?

The financial problems that beset the Port Olry project are more complex social indicators, partly because the villagers' ties with the marketplace are much stronger than in Longana, and partly because resistance to the government has always been more pronounced in Port Olry than almost anywhere else in Vanuatu. This resistance extends to the Fisheries Department; yet it is not a resistance to the marketplace. To the contrary, Port Olry villagers oppose the intervention of the Fisheries Department in what they see as a free market. If self-reliance means maintenance of their options, then the Fisheries Department seems to infringe on their self-reliance. For them the price alone is the captain. They want to be free to seek the best price for their fish, to sell where they wish, and to do something else if they don't feel like fishing. Many Port Olry fishermen are simply unwilling to exhibit the loyalty that the department feels is essential to the development of commercial fishing in Vanuatu. So their support of Remre is intermittent and weakened by social problems that pit the management of the fishing association and the fishermen against each other.

Is the Port Olry project a success? When I lived in Port Olry, Remre Fishing Association was losing money and the fishermen were "on strike" part of the time because of dissatisfaction with the manager. The attribute of Remre that made it a showcase of development for the Fisheries Department, was a negative asset in local opinion; the cold room and 15 boats looked impressive to Japanese aid donors, but the business was amounting to very little financially. This is quite the opposite of the Melanesian model of success whereby the greatest accomplishments come from the least obvious quarter.

Another negative aspect of the Port Olry project concerns the women who used to sell fresh fish at the Luganville market. As the Canadian volunteer who first talked to Celia Sarsom about a fishing association warned her would be the case, the produce market in Santo no longer allows the sale of fresh fish. Not only does this protect the health of local consumers of fish, it ensures that town residents hungry to buy fresh fish will wander over to Santofish, the government fish store on the fringes of the produce market. The women who used to sell fresh fish now prepare cooked fish, which they can still sell legally at the market. On a Friday night before the big Saturday market, the kitchens of market women in Port Olry exude the good smells of frying *mangru* cooked over open fires in restaurant-sized pots.

Yet Remre's poor financial picture, the strife over management of the association, and its impact on market women should not distract attention from its more positive consequences. Individuals have benefitted financially from Remre's presence in the village. For example, one fisherman was able to finance his new house from the sales of fish he caught using his brother's outboard motor boat. Unlike most owners, the brother allowed the fisherman to sell the catch to Remre in his own name and did not exact a percentage of the sale as rent for the boat. Thus, the fisherman was able to keep all of his income for himself. Nevertheless, everyone was surprised when the fisherman financed the construction of his new house entirely from fish sales. He bought timber, cement, and other building materials, and paid local boys to construct the house all with money earned from fish. Local admiration for this accomplishment reflects the cultural value placed on unexpected achievement, on wealth amidst apparent humility, or on things that are much greater than they seem to be at first glance. In this sense, the individual's achievement was the opposite of Remre's.

To most people in Port Olry, the fishing project has not made a great deal of difference. Even when I stayed with Celia, fishing was not a frequent topic of conversation. She and her household expressed far more interest in both soccer teams and copra prices than in commercial fishing. But this is, I think, a sign of the project's success rather than an indication of failure.

It would be inappropriate to expect a small fishing project based on simple technology to have a major social or economic impact on a community as economically active as Port Olry. The development of village fisheries in Vanuatu depends on slow, steady change that does not disrupt traditional lifestyles, and on the persistence of small projects. The Port Olry village fisheries development project measures up to these standards quite well. It is a good example of the positive impact that simple innovations, such as handreels, can have when introduced by an effective volunteer.

On the whole, the project has the potential to attract sufficient numbers of participants to make it economically and socially viable. Moreover, the project has been able to withstand periods in which, when the fishermen are "on strike" there is a temporary shift away from commercial fishing. With gardens to provide subsistence, with other, more lucrative, cash producing activities available, and without loans to repay, Port Olry fishermen can also be farmers, storekeepers, and truckdrivers. Fishing has added a new option to a traditional pattern of shifting between productive activities.

This option increases villagers' self-reliance, and in that sense, Remre is certainly a success. This is the criteria that was most important to the CUSO cooperant who served in Port Olry. Ken Ford felt that the project could be considered a success by the time he left because local people had the equipment and expertise that would allow them to earn substantial incomes from fishing. Even if people only used this equipment from time to time, in Ken's view, the project was successful. He told me, "Even though the income from the project has declined since I left, that is not a valid measure of success. The point is they have the access to fish. They have the choice to fish or not."

Individual fishermen benefit from the option to fish, but the fishing association itself bears the social and economic costs of periods of low fishing effort. Lack of consistent support for the association from fishermen, and the precarious financial situation created by a narrow profit margin and high costs have hindered the project in the past and are likely to continue to pose problems.

The most obvious effect of the project is the dramatic increase in the number of fishing boats on the Port Olry beach. But more significant are the less visible changes that flow from the acquisition of new boats. The addition of 15 fishing boats to the Port Olry fleet in less than 3 years is an impressive accomplishment, but Port Olry is a large village, and despite the community's unusual prosperity relatively few men have the wherewithal to buy a boat. On the surface it might seem that the fishing association has encouraged social differentiation between boat owners, captains, and crew because boat owners often do not fish and many fishermen do not own their own boats; but I don't think this is really the case. Indeed, one of Remre's most positive consequences has been the broad distribution of benefits among villagers following a traditional pattern in which wealthy older men provide less affluent, younger relatives and neighbors with capital assistance that allows them to become involved in an income producing activity.

Those who have benefitted most from the project are those who had the least when the project began. Female household heads now have greater access to fresh fish. Young men now have more income-generating options from which to choose. Canoe fishermen now have a market for any surplus they may catch.

The people of Port Olry have a long tradition of being independent and strong willed. Remre is an expression of these traits in both their positive and negative aspects. So long as Port Olry people continue to keep the government at arm's length, which they show every sign of doing, Remre will continue to reflect the tenor of life in the village, and of the relations between the village and the state. It will continue to represent, on the one hand, local people's desire for the wealth, material goods, and expertise that the government can provide and, on the other, their dislike of interference in local affairs.

Options and Constraints

Islanders have been able to maintain a kind of self-reliance that provides them with options regarding participation in the market. In this sense, their view of self-reliance converges with that of the CUSO cooperants and, to a more limited extent, with that of the Fisheries Department. They have the choice to go fishing or not, a choice that the volunteers endorse. They have the wherewithal to maintain a permanent fishing business, an option that the department would like to see them pursue. Through the simple commodity form of production, islanders enter into the capitalist marketplace on their own terms, as well as on terms that the market defines. They have the choice to participate or to opt out of production for the market because each household retains a large measure of control over its own means of production. The decision to work for money is only one alternative in the allocation of household labor, and it is one that need not be chosen as frequently as in other commodity-producing societies, given the rich natural environment of Vanuatu and the strength of kin-based "social security." Further, the decision to fish is only one of a range of cash-producing activities that is particularly wide in Port Olry. For most ni-Vanuatu, coconuts continue to provide the easiest route to an intermittent cash income, despite an overall downward trend in copra prices.

But what about the constraints that the state's development strategy imposes on people in the rural areas? Why doesn't the national goal of self-reliance take precedence when it conflicts with the islanders'? Indeed, anthropologists devote considerable attention these days to documenting the resistance and relative autonomy of rural people, but in order to understand how contradictions between national and local interests are worked out in practice, one needs to consider why the constraints of capitalism are not made more constraining in a particular situation.

First, let us consider the constraints imposed on islanders by the capitalist dimensions of village fisheries development. The requirement that an islander make a personal contribution of 10 percent of the project costs is a one time payment that does not place further liens on his labor. So the first real constraint facing an islander who takes on a fishing project is often the repayment of a loan. The

Development Bank allows borrowers three years in which to repay the principal of the loan as well as a 4 percent service charge. Loans for the early projects, which used more expensive boats than recent ones, were about $4,000. This meant, for example, that the Longana fishing project had to make quarterly payments of nearly $400.

The terms of Development Bank loans could be much more stringent, but this would defeat the purpose of the bank which was established in 1979 to encourage involvement in business opportunities on the part of islanders who lack capital and who cannot meet the size and/or security requirements of commercial banks. The government recognized that frequent defaults would be one consequence of efforts to stimulate local entrepreneurial activity in this way, commenting in the first national development plan that "the Bank will continue to take high risks in granting many small loans on which the security is minimal and its loan programme will, due to the nature of its operations, be costly to administer."[6] Foreign aid donors have provided the capital requirements of the Development Bank, which were estimated to be $1.4 million in 1986. Lack of applications has proved to be a major constraint on the bank's activity and has encouraged the persistence of easy terms as an incentive for borrowers.

A second constraint that fisheries development places on islanders is the obligation to file regular reports that demonstrate the project's level of fishing activity. Only by filing these reports, can a project obtain duty-free fuel. Such fuel, at about 35 cents/litre in October 1985, is about half the price of gasoline bought on the open market. Few projects can afford to fish without duty-free fuel, yet the obligation to file reports in order to get fuel brings with it the obligation to go fishing regularly, in order to show that one needs fuel.

With such a narrow margin between profit and loss in most projects, the fisheries department plays a crucial financial role. That role consists largely of attracting the investment of aid donors in the VFDP. There is virtually no attempt on the government's part to discover whether a particular project would be able to stand on its own financially. Fuel subsidies, grants, loans, a favorable price at the fish market, the expertise of an expatriate volunteer all help to create an image of success for the VFDP. They also make fishing projects imitations of "real" businesses. This image is, in a sense, more important than the bottom line on a realistic balance sheet, for the image of success is what attracts more aid.

It has been relatively easy to attract aid donors to support the program because they can see clearly how their money is put to use; they applaud the fact that the program directly reaches the village level and that it seems to have clear benefits to rural islanders, along with no obvious costs. For example, there is the "tourist route" which provides a pleasant day trip for potential aid donors who can visit picturesque beaches, inspect the installation at Port Olry, and return to the comfort of a hotel room in the town of Luganville by nightfall. There is the cargo that arrives partly because it is so much easier for the Fisheries Department to obtain aid earmarked for capital equipment (especially from Japan) than to acquire the services of experienced fishermen who could revitalize a failing fishing business.[7]

The nature of islanders' participation in the VFDP is such that the Fisheries Department has considerable leeway in presenting its public image to potential supporters of the program. Intermittent fishing effort throughout the rural sector means that wide swings are evident in productivity. It is easy for the department to emphasize the high points, regarding them as potential fishing levels in the archipelago. A single bonanza catch, such as Port Olry achieved in January 1984, is enough to encourage aid donors to greater participation in the program—for example, the donation of a coldroom—although it may not be enough to persuade local fishermen to engage in a consistent effort, day in and day out.

The Port Olry fishing association, then, takes on an importance for the state that is greater than its moderate influence on the community in which it is located. The Fisheries Department, in a sense, needs Port Olry more than the local people need the fishing project. The local people have other ways of earning money; they can afford to withdraw from commercial fishing either to go on strike against prevailing social or economic conditions, or to devote time to other activities. But, for the department, Port Olry provides a rare, almost experimental opportunity to explore the problems and prospects of making a market in premium-quality fish.

Prospects for the Future

So far, the carrot rather than the stick has been the government's approach to increasing the productivity of the rural sector. This seems likely to continue under the democratically elected government. Taxation of islanders is not a major source of government revenue, nor is it likely to be. Indigenous opposition to taxation has deep historical roots, and local governments still encounter some resistance to payment of a minimal head tax. On a national level, the country is a tax haven for foreign business, with no income taxes, corporate taxes or profits taxes and no controls on repatriation of profits. There are no immediate plans to introduce a system of direct taxation.

Incentives to increase rural islanders' involvement in commercial fishing activity are designed to increase catches, thereby, moving Vanuatu closer to the national goal of self-reliance. Unless more islanders go fishing more regularly, the image of success that the VFDP has created through cargo, subsidies, loans and encouragement will prove to be an illusion. With more regular fishing activity on the part of islanders, participation in a capitalist market for fish might be viable without the need for some fishermen to enter a capitalist mode of production. But, as we have seen, this increase in activity is unlikely to occur so long as islanders depend for their own self-reliance on keeping their options open.

The contradictions between the simple commodity economy and the kind of capitalist enterprise conventionally associated with the supply of urban markets mean that the development of a second generation of commercial fishermen cannot occur simply as an extension of the existing VFDP; but plans for moving along to this stage in developing Vanuatu's fishing industry are well-underway. Diesel powered boats ten m in length with facilities for sleeping on board are the first step. Loans for such vessels are large enough to oblige a captain to take fishing seriously. The operating costs are such that regular, productive effort is a necessity. The prototype of this boat was built at the Santo boatyard in 1985; although it sank as a result of a collision during it maiden trials, other such vessels are now in operation.

In conclusion, the VFDP is one particular example of the contradictory forces expressed in fishing where islanders meet the state in the same way as the coral reef breaks yet is pounded by sea. But there are many species of snapper that live in the same deep water world; the VFDP is only one of many similar fish in the sea of development. That one fish hauled up from the depths can teach us about the characteristics of others; but this book has been written in the belief that if instead, like a diver, we go where that fish lives, we can learn much more about the forces and beings that affect it, about what nourishes or weakens it, about where it is going and why.

Notes

1. Particularly profound social changes are required to make the idea of taxation palatable. Although I was especially aware of antipathy to taxes in Port Olry, because of the fear that I was there to impose a tax on fish, Longanans also resent and would like to oppose the idea of taxes on just about anything.

2. Moreover, the VFDP provides rural people who have moved to town with a form of investment that cements ties with their family in the islands. A guarantor is necessary in order to secure a Development Bank loan. People

with salaries can serve as guarantors for rural residents who want to start fishing projects. Often those who work in town help their rural relatives financially and assist them in dealing with the Fisheries Department to establish a project.

3. It is obviously different from agricultural activity in so many ways (Alexander 1982; Firth 1975) that I would not want to press the analogy between fishing and cash crops very far, except insofar as both are incorporated similarly into the simple commodity economy.

4. This is also the point of Sitiveni Halapua's study, *Fishermen of Tonga* (1982).

5. This was pointed out to me by a CUSO fisheries cooperant, but Rowena Lawson (1985) makes the same point in her book on fisheries development.

6. Vanuatu (1982:85).

7. "Japan's main problem in responding to calls to dispense more aid in the South Pacific is not finding the money—a little goes a long way among its small nations—but in getting recipient governments to think of acceptable ways to spend it." *Far Eastern Economic Review* (2 Oct 86) 134(40):26.

APPENDIX:
FINANCIAL ASSESSMENT
OF REMRE

Profitability

Although Remre is large in comparison to other VFDP projects, it is small enough to be a fragile business venture with only a narrow range between turning a reasonable profit and operating at a loss. The cost of purchasing fish must be kept below 72 percent and expenses must be held to 23 percent of sales revenue for the association to make a modest 5 percent profit under current conditions.

Even with careful attention to the monthly financial situation, seemingly minor variations in operating costs can make the difference between profit and loss. For example, the difference between September's profit and April's loss (see Figure 7) consists of only $70 in ice and $90 in miscellaneous expenses.[1]

Fish Purchasing Costs

The relative cost of fish purchases is a contentious issue. Fishermen complain that Remre pays too little for their fish. The manager feels that the prices he receives from Santofish are not high enough for the association to make a satisfactory profit. For example, in September 1985, Port Olry fishermen received an average price of 96.5 cents/kg for fish sold to Remre. The average price that Remre received from Santofish was $1.27/kg. Thus Remre was paying an unacceptably high 76 percent of sales revenue to buy fish. Rather than lower the price paid to fishermen, which might have resulted in their ceasing to fish commercially altogether, the manager found a buyer who would pay more than Santofish; he sold 650 kg of fish to Chinese buyers for about $1.53/kg.

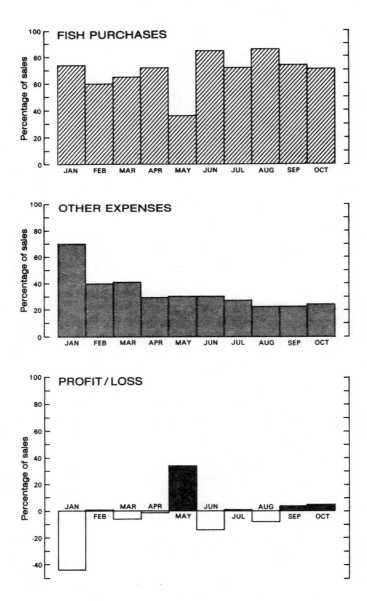

Remre Fishing Association
FISH PURCHASES, OTHER EXPENSES AND PROFIT/LOSS
AS A PERCENTAGE OF SALES FOR JAN-OCT 1985

FIGURE 7

Operating Expenses

Operating expenses have always been high at Remre, and it seems unlikely that they can be reduced below about 22 percent of sales under current conditions. Ken Ford attempted to reduce the cost of transporting fish to Santofish, but transport remains the largest monthly expense when the association is running well. Port Olry trucks consume about $20 in fuel (at private pump rates) to make one round trip from the village to Luganville; the usual charge for making the trip is $35, which seems a reasonable rate considering the cost of fuel, the driver's wages, and depreciation on the vehicle.

Results of the study indicate that transport can be as much as 50 percent of total operating expenses without cause for concern. The crucial constraint is that transport costs should not exceed 11 percent of sales revenue. As Figure 8 shows, "miscellaneous" expenses vary considerably from month to month. The business runs best if miscellaneous expenses are kept to about 10 percent of total expenses. The data for March in Figure 8 demonstrate that miscellaneous expenses can easily swallow potential monthly profits.

Potential Earnings

Remre's actual loss as a percentage of sales for Jan-Oct 1985 was 1 percent or $237.77. If instead the association had made a 5 percent profit, it would have earned $935.37 or almost $1160.00 more than it did. A 5 percent profit means that Remre makes only about 7 cents per kg of fish compared to the 40 cent/kg profit realized in the first year of operation; but this rate of

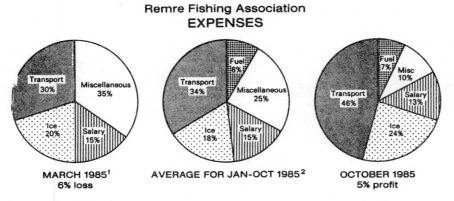

Remre Fishing Association
EXPENSES

MARCH 1985[1]
6% loss

AVERAGE FOR JAN-OCT 1985[2]

OCTOBER 1985
5% profit

[1] no fuel costs in March
[2] data missing for May

FIGURE 8

profit can be sufficient to maintain a viable business under good management.

Remre's projected annual sales, based on the first ten months of 1985, were $22,452. If the association made a profit of 5 percent on these sales, it would earn $1123. It seemed to me that Remre should be able to achieve such a profit under current conditions in 1986 if monthly expenses were carefully monitored. If Remre could once again handle 1.6 tonnes of fish per month, as it did in its first year of operation, profits (at 7 cents/kg) would rise to about $1344. This would provide enough income to pay an adequate dividend to shareholders, even if confidence in Remre increased and more fishermen chose to participate in the project as shareholders than had been the case previously.

Notes

1. The data for May in Figure 1 are anomalous. The volume of fish purchased was low, expenses were about average, but the rate of profit soared. The reason is that in April the Fisheries Department asked Port Olry fishermen to catch 1 tonne of snapper for export trials to England. These fish were not entered in the daily records, because it was an exceptional event; but the money paid for the fish was recorded when it was received in May.

BIBLIOGRAPHY

Adams, R. (1984) *In the Land of Strangers*. Canberra: RSPacS.

Alexander, P. (1982) *Sri Lankan Fishermen*. Canberra: ANU Monographs on SE Asia.

Amarshi, A., K. Good, and R. Mortimer (1979) *Development and Dependency: The Political Economy of Papua New Guinea*. Melbourne: Oxford University Press.

Asia 1984 Yearbook. *Far Eastern Economic Review: Special Issue*.

Beasant, J. (1984) *The Santo Rebellion: An Imperial Reckoning*. Honolulu: Univ of Hawaii Press.

Bergin, A. (1983) "Fisheries in the South Pacific." *Asia Pacific Quarterly* 22: 20–32.

Blackburn, D. (1985) *Fishing Boats in Vanuatu*. Ottawa: CUSO.

Bodley, J.H. (1975) *Victims of Progress*. Menlo Park, CA: Cummings.

Bonnemaison, J. (1985) "The Tree and the Canoe: Roots and Mobility in Vanuatu Societies." In M. Chapman (ed): *Pacific Viewpoint*. Special Issue "Mobility and Identity in the Island Pacific."

Bonnemaison, J. (1986) *La Derniére Ile*. Paris: ARLEA/ORSTOM.

Bourdieu, P. (1977) *Outline of a Theory of Practice*. Cambridge: Cambridge University Press.

Brookfield, H.C., with D. Hart (1971) *Melanesia: A Geographical Interpretation of an Island World*. London: Methuen.

Brouard, F., and R. Grandperrin (1985) *Deep-Bottom Fishes of the Outer Reef Slope in Vanuatu*. Port Vila: ORSTOM.

Brunton, R. (1979) "Kava and the Daily Dissolution of Society on Tanna." *Mankind* 12: 93–103.

Chayanov, A.V. (1966) *The Theory of Peasant Economy*. Homewood, IL: American Economic Assoc.

Chevalier, J. (1982) *Civilization and the Stolen Gift: Capital, Kin and Cult in Eastern Peru*. Toronto: Univ of Toronto Press.

Cillaurren, E., and G. David (1986) *ORSTOM Participation in the 3rd*

Workshop on the Development of Village Fisheries in Vanuatu. Port Vila: ORSTOM.

Connell, J. (1982) "Development and Dependency: Divergent Approaches to the Political Economy of Papua New Guinea." In R.J. May and H. Nelson (eds.), *Melanesia: Beyond Diversity*. Canberra: RSPacS, pp. 501-527.

Connell, J. (1983) "Migration, Employment and Development in the South Pacific." *Country Report* No. 20. Noumea: South Pacific Commission.

Corris, P. (1970) "Pacific Island Labour Migrants in Queensland." *Journal of Pacific History* 5: 43–64.

Couper, A. (1986) "New Maritime Technology—The Social Dimension." A paper prepared for a workshop on New Marine Technology and Social Change in the Pacific. Canberra: ANU.

Crossland, J. (1984a) *The Vanuatu Village Fisheries Development Programme*. Port Vila: Fisheries Dept.

Crossland, J. (1984b) *Port Vila Fisheries Ltd: The Establishment and Operation of a Government Owned Fish Marketing Company*. Port Vila: Fisheries Dept.

David, G. (1985) "La Peche Villageoise à Vanuatu: Recensement 1—Moyens de Production et Production Globale." *Notes et Documents d'Oceanographie* No.12. Port Vila: Mission Orstom.

David, G. (1986) "Consumption of Sea Produce and Marketing." In E. Cillaurren and G. David (eds.), *ORSTOM Participation in the 3rd Workshop on the Development of Village Fisheries in Vanuatu*. Port Vila: ORSTOM, pp. 18–25.

Douglas, M. with M. Micod (1974) "Taking the Biscuit: The Structure of British Meals." *New Society* 30:744–747.

Durrenberger, E.P., ed. (1984) *Chayanov, Peasants, and Economic Anthropology*. Orlando: Academic Press.

Emmerson, D.K. (1983) "Rethinking Artisanal Fisheries Development: Western Concepts and Asian Experience." *World Bank Staff Working Paper No. 423*. Washington, D.C.: World Bank.

Epple, G. (1977) "Technological Change in a Grenada, W.I. Fishery, 1950–1970." In E.M. Smith (ed.): *Those Who Live from the Sea*. St. Paul: West, pp. 173–194.

Finney, B. (1973a) *Big Men and Business: Entrepreneurship and Economic Growth in the New Guinea Highlands*. Honolulu: University of Hawaii Press.

Finney, B. (1973b) *Polynesian Peasants and Proletarians*. Cambridge, MA: Schenkman.

Firth, R. (1975) *Malay Fishermen: Their Peasant Economy*. New York: Norton.

Fitzpatrick, P. (1980) *Law and State in Papua New Guinea*. Toronto: Academic Press.

Friedmann, H. (1980) "Household Production and the National Economy: Concepts for the Analysis of Agrarian Formations." *Journal of Peasant Studies* 7 (2): 158–184.

Gilding, M. (1982) "The Massacre of the Mystery." *Journal of Pacific History* 17(2): 66–85.

Gopalakrishnan, C., ed. (1984) *The Emerging Marine Economy of the Pacific.* Boston: Butterworth.

Gregory, C.A. (1982) *Gifts and Commodities.* Toronto: Academic Press.

Haberkorn, G. (1985) "Recent Population Trends in Vanuatu." *Islands/Australia Working Paper* No.85/4. National Centre for Development Studies. Canberra:ANU.

Halapua, S. (1982) *Fishermen of Tonga.* Suva, Fiji: University of the South Pacific.

Hammel, E.A., and P. Laslett (1974) "Comparing Household Structure Over Time and Between Cultures." *Comparative Studies in Society and History* 16: 73–109.

Howlett, D. (1973) "Terminal Development: From Tribalism to Peasantry." In H.C. Brookfield (ed.), *The Pacific in Transition.* London: Edward Arnold.

Hung, M. (1983) *National Nutrition Survey Report.* Port Vila: Dept of Health.

Hyden, G. (1980) *Beyond Ujaama in Tanzania.* London: Heinemann.

Hyden, G. (1983) *No Shortcuts to Progress: African Development Management in Perspective.* London: Heineman.

Ifeka, C. (1986) "Why Women Count: Prospects for Self-Reliant Fisheries Development in the South Pacific Compared to the Indian Ocean." A paper presented to A. Couper's workshop on Fisheries Development, The Australian National University. MSS.

Jardin, C., and J. Crosnier (1975) *Un Taro, Un Poisson, Une Papaye.* Noumea: SPC.

Jolly, M. (1982) "Birds and Banyans of South Pentecost: Kastom in Anticolonial Struggle." In Keesing, R. and R. Tonkinson (eds.), *Reinventing Traditional Culture: The Politics of Kastom in Island Melanesia, Mankind* (Special Issue) 13(4): 338–356.

Kahn, J. (1980) *Minangkabau Social Formations.* Cambridge: Cambridge University Press.

Kahn, J. (1985) "Peasant Ideologies in the Third World." *Annual Reviews in Anthropology* 14: 49–75.

Kasfir, N. (1986) "Are African Peasants Self-Sufficient?" *Development and Change* 17: 335–357.

Keesing, R. (1976) *Cultural Anthropology: A Contemporary Perspective.* New York: Holt, Rinehart and Winston (2nd Edition, 1981).

Lane, R. (1971) "New Hebrides: Land Tenure without Land Policy." In R. Crocombe (ed.), *Land Tenure in the Pacific.* Melbourne: Oxford University Press.

Lawson, R. (1985) *Economics of Fisheries Development.* London: Frances Pinter.

Leap, W. (1977) "Maritime Subsistence in Anthropological Perspective: A Statement of Priorities." In M.E. Smith (ed.), *Those Who Live From the Sea.* St. Paul: West.

LeBrun, O., and C. Gerry (1975) "Petty Producers and Capitalism." *Review of African Political Economy* 3: 20-32.

Liklik Buk (1986) Liklik Buk Information Centre. Lae, Papva New Guinea: Melanesian Council of Churches.

Lindstrom, L. (ed.) (1987) "Drugs in Western Pacific Societies." *ASAO*, Vol. 11. Lanham, MD: University Press of America.

MacClancy, J. (1981) *To Kill a Bird with Two Stones: A Short History of Vanuatu.* Port Vila: Vanuatu Cultural Centre.

McGee, T.G., R.G. Ward, and D.W. Drakakis-Smith (1980) *Food Distribution in the New Hebrides.* ANU Development Centre. Monograph No. 25. Canberra: ANU.

Meggitt, M. (1971) "From Tribesmen to Peasants: the Case of the Mae Enga of New Guinea." In L.R. Hiatt and C. Jayawardena (eds.), *Anthropology in Oceania.* Sydney: Angus and Robertson.

Philibert, J.-M. (1986) "The Politics of Tradition; Toward a Generic Culture in Vanuatu." *Mankind* 16: 1–12.

Philibert, J.-M. (1988) "Consuming Culture: A Study of Simple Commodity Consumption." In B. Orlove and H. Rutz (eds.), *The Social Economy of Consumption.* Lanham, MD: University Press of America.

Quille, H. (1985) *Enquetes sur l'Emploi en 1983: le Secteur Privé Urbain.* Port Vila: NPSO.

Ridings, P.J. (1983) *Resource Use Arrangements in Southwest Pacific Fisheries.* Honolulu: East-West Center.

Rodman, M. (1977) Kanaka Connection. MSS.

Rodman, M. (1981) *Customary Illusions: Land and Copra in Longana, Vanuatu.* Ph.D. dissertation. Hamilton, Canada: McMaster University.

Rodman, M. (1983) "Following Peace: Indigenous Pacification of a Northern New Hebridean Society." In M. Rodman and M. Cooper, (eds.), *The Pacification of Melanesia.* ASAO Monograph No. 7. Lanham, MD: University Press of America.

Rodman, M. (1984) "Masters of Tradition: Customary Land Tenure and New Forms of Social Inequality in a Vanuatu Peasantry." *American Ethnologist* 11(1): 61–80.

Rodman, M. (1985a) "Contemporary Custom: Redefining Domestic Space in Longana, Vanuatu." *Ethnology* 24 (4): 269–279.

Rodman, M. (1985b) "Moving Houses: Residential Mobility and the Mobility of Residences in Longana, Vanuatu." *American Anthropologist* 87: 56–72.

Rodman, M. (1986) *Remre Fishing Association: A Socio-Economic Evaluation.* Prepared for CUSO Vanuatu, February.

Rodman, M. (1987a) "Constraining Capitalism? Contradictions of Self-Reliance in Vanuatu Fisheries Development." *American Ethnologist* 14 (4): 108–122.

Rodman, M. (1987b) "Enracinement de l'Identité: La Tenure Fonciere à Longana, Vanuatu." *Culture* VI(2): 3–11.

Rodman, M. (1987c) *Masters of Tradition.* Vancouver: UBC Press.

Rodman, M., and W. Rodman (1983) "The 100 Days of Sara Mata: Explaining Unnatural Death in Vanuatu." In P. Stephenson (ed), *Cross-Cultural Studies of Death and Dying.* (Special Issue) OMEGA 14(3):135–144.

Rodman, W. (1979) "Big Men and Middlemen: The Politics of Law in Longana." *American Ethnologist* 4: 525–537.

Rodman, W. (1985) " 'A Law Unto Themselves': Legal Innovation in Ambae, Vanuatu." *American Ethnologist* 4: 603–622.

Rodman, W. L., and M. Rodman (1985) "On the Politics of Place Naming in Vanuatu." *Oceania* 55: 242–251.

Rodman, W. L., and M. Rodman (n.d.) "To Die on Ambae: On the Possibility of Doing Fieldwork Forever." Manuscript.

Roseberry, W. (1985) "The Ideology of Domestic Production." A paper prepared for the American Ethnological Society Annual Meeting. Toronto.

Sahlins, M. (1972) *Stone Age Economics*. London: Tavistock.

Scarr, D. (1967a) *Fragments of Empire: A History of the Western Pacific High Commission, 1877–1914*. Canberra: Australian National University Press.

Scarr, D. (1967b) "Recruits and Recruiters." *Journal of Pacific History* 2: 15-24.

Schoeffel, P. (1985) "Women in the Fisheries of the South Pacific. In H. Hughes (ed), *Women in Development in the South Pacific*. Canberra: Development Studies Center, pp. 156–175.

Shears, R. (1980) "The Coconut War." Melbourne: Cassell.

Shineberg, D. (1967) *They Came for Sandalwood: A Study of the Sandalwood Trade in the South-West Pacific, 1830–1865*. Melbourne: Melbourne University Press.

Smillie, I. (1985) *The Land of Lost Content: A History of CUSO*. Toronto: Deneau.

Smith, C.A. (1984a) "Does a Commodity Economy Enrich the Few While Ruining the Masses? Differentiation Among Petty Commodity Producers in Guatemala." *Journal of Peasant Studies* 11 (3): 60–95.

Smith, C.A. (1984b) "Forms of production in Practice: Fresh Approaches to Simple Commodity Production." *Journal of Peasant Studies*: 200–221.

Smith, M.E. (ed.) (1977) *Those Who Live from the Sea*. St. Paul: West.

Stanley, D. (1986) *South Pacific Handbook*. Chico, CA: Moon Publications.

Strathern, A. (1975) "By Toil or Guile? The Uses of Coils and Crescents by Tolai and Hagen Big Men." *Journal de la Société des Océanistes* 49: 363–378.

Swerdloff, S. (1984) "Hawaii's Fisheries: An Overview." In C. Gopalkrishnan (ed), *The Emerging Marine Economy in the Pacific*. Boston: Butterworth, pp. 121–144.

Vanuatu (1982) *The First National Development Plan, 1982–1986*. Port Vila: National Planning Office.

Vanuatu (1983) *Report on the Census of the Population, 1979*. Port Vila: NPSO.

Vanuatu (1984a) *The Mid-Term Review of Vanuatu's First National Development Plan*. Port Vila: NPSO.

Vanuatu (1984b) *Fisheries Department Annual Report*. Port Vila: Fisheries Dept.

Vanuatu (1984c) *Vanuatu in Figures*. Port Vila: NPSO.

Vanuatu (1986) "Ol Risalt Blon Sensas Blong Taon." *Tam Tam* (22 March).

Vercruijsse, E. (1984) *The Penetration of Capitalism: A West African Case Study*. London: Zed Books.

Wolf, E. (1982) *Europe and the People Without History*. Berkeley: University of California Press.

INDEX